De Oratione

De Oratione

HUMBERT OF ROMANS
(1200–1277)

A Collection of his Writings on PRAYER
—— FROM HIS ——
Commentary on the Rule of St Augustine,
the *Commentary on the Constitutions*
of the Order of Preachers,
& On Duties

Translated from the Latin *by*
FR THOMAS CREAN, O.P.

Introduction by
FR GREGORY SCHNAKENBERG, O.P.

AROUCA
PRESS

Originally published at Santa Sabina (Dominican General Curia in Rome) in 1960 as no. 1 in the Series *Bibliotheca Dominicana*. Fr Hyacinth M. Hering, O.P., was the compiler.

Thomas Crean is a Dominican friar of the Province of England.

Scripture quotations are taken from the Douay-Rheims translation, with minor modifications when necessary to better approximate the Latin text employed by Humbert of Romans.

ISBN: 978-1-989905-24-1 (pbk)
ISBN: 978-1-989905-25-8 (hardcover)

Arouca Press
PO Box 55003
Bridgeport PO
Waterloo, ON N2J3G0
Canada
www.aroucapress.com
Send inquiries to info@aroucapress.com

Book and cover design by
Michael Schrauzer

CONTENTS

INTRODUCTION

ALTHOUGH BELONGING TO A TRADITION spanning over eight hundred years, few Dominican friars have had a wider range of influence on the shape of Dominican life, liturgy, and spirituality than Humbert of Romans (c. 1200–77). While often overshadowed by his more well-known Dominican contemporaries, including Thomas Aquinas, Albert the Great, and Hugh of St. Cher, Humbert's role as Master of the Dominican Order from 1254 to 1263 and his considerable body of writings helped to firmly establish the way of life inaugurated by St. Dominic in 1216.

A native of the Burgundy region of France, Humbert first met the friars as a student at the University of Paris and ultimately decided to leave behind the prospect of an academic career for the sake of entering the Order, which he did in 1224. His talents and capacities for leadership must have been quickly recognized — for he rose quickly through the ranks of conventual lector, then Prior, then Provincial of the Roman Province, followed by Provincial of the French Province, and eventually Master of the Order in 1254. Thus throughout the mid-thirteenth century, Humbert was in a unique position to both observe and contribute to the Dominican Order's early flourishing. Yet despite having been a prolific author throughout much of this period, Humbert's writings remain largely untranslated and unknown except to specialists in medieval and Dominican history. Happily, this present volume now offers, for the first time, a collection of Humbert's writings on prayer in an accessible English translation.

The Present Work

ALTHOUGH HUMBERT DID NOT WRITE A SPE-cific treatise on prayer, the practice of prayer occupied a significant part of his own life as a Dominican friar and thus naturally appears as a topic of consideration within his writings. In the mid-twentieth century, Fr. Hyacinth Hering, O.P., who served as a professor at the Pontifical University of St. Thomas Aquinas (the Angelicum) in Rome, undertook to compile Humbert's various thoughts on prayer, which were scattered across his different works. In particular, Fr. Hering brought together Humbert's writings on prayer from his *Commentary on the Constitutions of the Order*, his *Commentary on the Rule of Augustine*, and his work *On Duties*. The first two of these were probably written in the late-1240s through the early 1250s, while the last was composed in the 1260s. To these, Fr. Herring also added a few testimonies taken from St. Dominic's canonization process that pertained to Dominic's own practice of prayer. He then rounded out the collection with some short extracts from the thirteenth-century Dominicans Jordan of Saxony and Gerard de Frachet concerning the early friars' zeal and devotion to prayer.

Fr. Hering's original compilation, which he titled *De Oratione*, was printed in Latin in 1960 and relied on the edition of Humbert's works edited by Fr. Joachim Joseph Berthier, O.P., in 1888–89. In fact, Berthier's edition remains the most current printed edition for some of Humbert's works, including his longest, the *Commentary on the Rule of Augustine*. Since most Dominicans and Catholic clergy were still accustomed to reading Latin handbooks in the early 1960s, Fr. Hering's little Latin collection of Humbert's writings on prayer still had a natural audience. Such, however, is no longer the case and both the majority of Humbert's writings and Fr. Hering's compilation are now largely inaccessible to clergy and laity alike.

Yet the present translation, prepared by Fr. Thomas Crean, O.P., helps to remedy this situation. It constitutes the first appearance in English of Fr. Hering's book and also the first appearance in English of most of Humbert's writings on prayer. It should certainly be welcomed not only by those interested in Dominican or medieval spirituality but also by any reader who wishes to know more about how Christians have prayed through the centuries and/or those looking for assistance or inspiration in their own spiritual life.

Humbert and the Form of Prayer

I T SHOULD PERHAPS BE SAID AT THE OUTSET that those seeking a specific 'method' or technique of prayer will not find this in Humbert's writings. While methods and techniques of mental prayer may be helpful, these concerns are more characteristic of later historical periods. Rather, for Humbert and his fellow medieval Dominicans, prayer consisted first and foremost in the regular and solemn celebration of the community's liturgy, which included both the daily conventual Mass and the chanted Divine Office. The latter was sung at regular intervals throughout the day and night, including the liturgical offices of matins and lauds that the friars celebrated in the earliest hours of the new day while it was still very dark. Humbert highlights this extremely early rising for these liturgical offices as one of the Order's notable penances, and likewise one that obtained many graces and blessings.

Although the liturgy of the Church formed the central core of the friars' prayers—and occupied a significant part of their day—the friars also offered personal prayers, which Humbert commonly calls 'secret prayers' since they were said in private (*in secreto*) rather than as part of a public liturgy. These private prayers would naturally take various forms, depending on the individual, but the seven penitential psalms (6, 32, 38, 51, 102, 130, and 143) were clearly a staple of the ordinary friar's prayer life. Likewise, intercessory prayer, offered both for personal needs and the needs of others, was characteristic of the friars' practice of prayer—something they saw as modelled within the "Our Father" itself.

Notwithstanding the absence of a specific method, Humbert does discuss at length what might hinder prayer or, alternatively, make it more effective. While Humbert attends to external matters such as time and place, he also shows himself a keen student of human nature and how body and soul influence each other. For example, when discussing the value of bowing profoundly in prayer—a regular practice of the friars—he remarks that "humility makes a prayer powerful, and so it is good for one who is praying to humble himself by bowing." Related observations about kneeling, genuflecting, prostrating oneself, and making the sign of the cross all appear in Humbert's writings.

While the physical dimensions of prayer receive due attention from Humbert, he does not therefore neglect its material content. Along with the traditional vocal prayers of the *Our Father*, *Hail Mary*, and *Glory Be*, Humbert also echoes a long line of saints before him in recommending the Psalter as a treasury of Christian prayer. As one who prayed the Divine Office regularly, Humbert knew firsthand how the rich language of the psalms could express a wide range of human emotions and desires. But more importantly, as Humbert observes, "more or less every verse speaks about God . . . and so with God being thus placed before our eyes, the mind is greatly lifted up to what is above."

While the psalms provide extensive content for both vocal and mental prayer, Humbert also considers the role of silent meditation and the wide variety of subjects one could fruitfully meditate upon. While providing an ample list of such topics and remarking upon the relationship of meditation to one's emotions, he also adds the important caveat: "these things are learned more by experience than by teaching." This does not mean, of course, that Humbert has no advice to offer. But for Humbert, skill in prayer is ultimately acquired in the same way that one acquires any good habit, that is, by repeated action. The repetition of the liturgy, private prayers, and meditation all coalesce to aid one in acquiring this habit—and to help the individual respond to God's grace as the true source and origin of all prayer. Complementing this, Humbert likewise speaks of Marian devotion and the aid Mary offers to those who turn to her as their patroness and helper. Not surprisingly, Humbert makes special reference to the *Salve regina* and its associated liturgical procession—a quintessentially Dominican practice—along with the prayers of the *Little Office of Our Lady*.

Humbert offers considerable encouragement and advice for those seeking holiness and greater devotion in prayer. But he also seeks to root out the vices that undermine prayer. Unconfessed sins, struggles with forgiveness and anger, and the way various interior states can render prayer unfruitful are all commented upon. Additionally, he challenges what he terms 'cherished anger,' which 'prevents prayer from obtaining the effect which is mercy.' Not infrequently, Humbert diagnoses problems that afflict the human heart and seeks to remedy them. But while seeking to remove the obstacles to prayer, he avoids mapping the path one's prayers might travel or providing a schema for the spiritual life. In that sense, Humbert's writings are more like practical advice than a work of spiritual or mystical theology. Yet, one might still observe that the way of life Humbert promoted and shared with his fellow friars produced its fair share of mystics, implying that the usefulness of his observations for the spiritual life should not be underestimated.

Humbert's Style and Sources

TAKEN AS A WHOLE, MUCH OF HUMBERT'S style can best be described as exhortative in nature. Undoubtably reflecting his own experience as a medieval preacher, Humbert usually proceeds by making a particular point and then by drawing together an abundance of quotations, examples, scripture citations, and other authorities to support his claim and to motivate the reader to greater holiness. While a contemporary reader might be tempted to judge these lists—or 'chains of authorities' as they are sometimes called—as excessive or redundant, medieval readers (and preachers) probably saw things differently. By drawing together so many supporting authorities, Humbert not only amplified his argument but also highlighted many different facets of a particular point, providing the reader with a mini-compendium of observations to meditate upon or to commit to memory. Of course, some examples or authorities would resonate more deeply with certain readers or listeners than others. But by providing a small treasury of references, it increased the likelihood that something might move one's heart and mind to greater devotion.

While Fr. Hering arranged *De Oratione* by compiling excerpts of Humbert's writings, one can nonetheless get a good sense of Humbert's own preferred authors and spiritual authorities even from this limited sampling. Perhaps unsurprisingly, Humbert quotes from Scripture far more than any other authority, relying on the Divine Word as the foundation for his claims and as the most effective resource for exhortation. Apart from Scripture, however, St. Bernard of Clairvaux (d. 1153), the venerated and extremely influential medieval Cistercian, clearly emerges as one of Humbert's most beloved authors. Indeed, Humbert's *Commentary on the Rule of Augustine* repeatedly turns to St. Bernard as a source for spiritual insight and illumination. Other sources that appear frequently include St. Augustine of Hippo (d. 430), St. Gregory the Great (d. 604), and the collected *Lives of the Fathers* (*Vitae Patrum*). Although less commonly, references are also made to the Jewish historian Josephus (d. c. 100), the bishop John Chrysostom (d. 407), the proto-encyclopedist St. Isidore of Seville (d. 636), the French theologian John Beleth (fl. 1135–82), and the Dominican Master Jordan of Saxony (d. 1237) among others. Humbert not only read widely, he also wove together the insights of those before him into a synthetic presentation — thus ensuring that the reader who had not encountered or read all these other authors might still benefit from some of their wisdom.

Concluding Thoughts

WHILE HUMBERT LARGELY WROTE FOR HIS own Dominican brothers, the surviving manuscripts suggest that at least some of his works were widely distributed and welcomed in many non-Dominican communities. His *Commentary on the Rule of Augustine*—excerpts from which form a significant part of this present work—survives in nearly 100 medieval manuscripts spread across libraries and religious communities in

Europe. Regardless of Humbert's target audience, many non-Dominicans clearly found his writings valuable. Indeed, there is much here to enliven the prayer life of anyone, regardless of their vocation, and regardless of whether they are a beginner or well-advanced in the spiritual life.

One might also add that students of medieval religious life and medieval history will undoubtably find some of Humbert's observations intriguing, perhaps even amusing, as he remarks on the friars' practices and habits. Along similar lines, those accustomed to a post-conciliar liturgical world with its stress on lauds and vespers as the two "hinges" of the liturgical day may find Humbert's emphasis on the offices of matins (with lauds), prime, and compline a bit surprising. Yet these were often the most difficult offices for friars to attend and Humbert's remarks serve as helpful reminders of how much Humbert's liturgical experience (and those of his fellow friars) differed from our own and how liturgical spirituality and its emphases can vary over time.

For a contemporary reader, Humbert's style can admittedly seem a bit moralizing at times. Yet his directness and willingness to diagnose faults can also be rather refreshing and salutary — provided one takes his observations in a spirit of charity (as indeed they were intended). For Humbert, salvation was achieved only by grace, but an effective word could nonetheless be a powerful instrument for helping to move one from mere potentiality to action. As a preacher, Humbert sought to do just that — and his writings on prayer reflect this desire to turn ever more hearts and minds toward God in prayer and devotion. One hopes that this new translation sees that desire further realized in our own day as well.

Fr. Gregory Schnakenberg, OP
August 8, 2020
Feast of St. Dominic

PART I

On Prayer & Meditation

I

On Prayer

1. Why religious should be devoted above others to prayers, especially at the appointed hours and seasons

ALTHOUGH EVERYONE SHOULD BE DEVOTED to prayer, insofar as it has been said to everyone, *Be constant in prayer* (Rom. 12:12), yet this especially applies to religious. For dwelling as they do among trials, since they cannot defend themselves without the help of the Most High, they should fervently invoke divine aid. *Watch ye, and pray that ye enter not into temptation* (Mt. 26:41).

Again, since according to Gregory the gifts of God are easily lost unless they are preserved by the Giver, anyone who has some gift of God must have recourse to the Giver, so that He may guard it; and the one who has more must have recourse more often. It was in this sense that Gregory taught the universal Church to pray in the prayer which says, "Guard in Thy new family the spirit of adoption which Thou hast given."[1]

Again, people especially call upon divine help in difficult matters, and so David, considering how difficult it is to go along the narrow road of the counsels unto the end, prayed, saying, *Perfect my steps in thy paths* (Ps. 64:5).

---

1 Humbert is quoting here a prayer used at the Paschal Vigil (Holy Saturday) liturgy.

[1]

Therefore, since religious are more beset by trials than others—for it is said, *Son, when thou comest to the service of God, stand in justice and in fear, and prepare thy soul for temptation* (Ecclus. 2:1)—and since they also have a greater share of heavenly gifts, and have before them a very difficult task, namely bringing a work of perfection to its fulfilment, there is upon them a threefold need to pray more than others, given the persistence of their trials, the ease with which their goods may be lost and the difficulty of their endeavour.

Moreover, the fewer tasks one has, the more opportunity one has for prayer. So it is said: *Let nothing hinder you from praying always* (Ecclus. 18:22), that is: "Do not take upon yourself those things that will hinder you from prayer", such as various tasks and affairs.

Again, a suitable place also favours prayer. *We will adore in the place where his feet stood* (Ps. 131:7).

Again, prayer is favoured by a holy and devout company, which says by word and example: *Come, let us adore and fall down before God* (Ps. 94:6).

Therefore, since religious have few activities taking them away from prayer, and dwell in a place very suited to it, and have company that draws them to it in many ways, they have a threefold opportunity for prayer, by reason of their freedom of spirit, their place and their society.

Moreover, the contemplative state carries with it an obligation to pray, since according to Bernard, prayer is a part of contemplation. *In Maspha was a place of prayer* (1 Mach. 3:46). 'Maspha' signifies contemplation.

Again, those who live from alms must pray for their benefactors, imitating Paul who prayed: *The Lord give mercy to the house of Onesiphorus: because he hath often refreshed me, and hath not been ashamed of my chain* (2 Tim. 1:16).

Again, just as rich men who are not able to pray much must make up for this want by almsgiving, ransoming their souls with much alms, even so those who cannot give alms must make up for this by their prayers. So, many people who are unable to give material things to the poor give them their prayers instead, in this way fulfilling the word: *Give to every one that asketh thee* (Lk. 6:30).

Thus, religious are greatly bound to persevere in prayer, since they are placed in the contemplative state, since nearly all that they have to sustain them has been given to them by those who hope thus to gain the benefit of their prayers, and since they are unable to give alms, having nothing of their own. Therefore, by reason of necessity, by reason of opportunity and by reason of a debt, they must be more devoted to prayer than others. This is clearly shown by this passage: *Cornelius, a religious man, always praying to God* (Acts 10:2).

Now although these men must be very dedicated to prayer, this especially applies to prayers at the appointed hours and seasons. For this is not simply a matter of prayer but also of obedience, as Lambert, the Abbot of St Rufus, says in his commentary on the Rule of Augustine. It is certain that a twofold good is better than a single one; so when obedience, which especially pleases God, is joined to prayer, this become even more acceptable to Him.

Again, not only one convent comes together to pray at the appointed hours and seasons, but a vast plethora throughout the world. So since, as the same authority says, it is impossible for the prayers of many to remain unanswered, everyone who comes to pray must hope that he will be speedily answered, if not in virtue of his own prayer, at least in virtue of the multitude then praying to which he unites himself.

Again, it is likely that just as prayers are more speedily answered when they are offered in a place set apart for prayer, according to the text: *My ears shall be attentive to the prayer of him that shall pray in this place* (2 Chron. 7:15), so it is likely that this is also true of a time established by the Holy Ghost, according to the text: *In an acceptable time I have heard thee, and in the day,* etc. (Is. 49:8).

Therefore, since the Church, which is governed by the Spirit of God, has established certain times and seasons for praying, it must be believed that those who then pray are the more speedily heard, just as the poor man who comes to the abbey to beg alms at the time fixed for this receives them more quickly than if he came at another time.

Commentary on the Rule of Augustine, c.45.

---

2. Why we should pray more keenly on feast days and on fast days and on Rogation days and at certain other times

IN REGARD TO FEAST DAYS, NOTE THAT ONE should be free from all work: *Thou shalt do no work on it* (Ex. 20:10).

Again, it is probable that on these days, since they are feasts of God, the King of heaven bestows gifts more abundantly, just as Assuerus in the feast for Esther's wedding *bestowed gifts according to princely magnificence* (Est. 2:18).

Again, on feast days, when God should be better served, demons are more troublesome to men. *Antiochus's army made war against the Jews on the sabbath day* (1 Mach. 2:32).

It is clear then that we must set about prayer more eagerly on feast days, since these days were instituted especially to be free for God, since our hope in the bounty of Him to whom we pray is greater then, and since the enemy troubles us more, and so is to be the more stoutly resisted by prayers.

An example of this was given to us of old. *We therefore at all times without ceasing, remember you in our festivals, in the sacrifices that we offer* (1 Mach. 12:11). It is noted in this place that prayers were particularly offered in the festivals.

With regard to fasts, note that just as fasting exists to sanctify us in opposition to bodily vices, so prayer does the same in regard to spiritual vices. Jerome says: "By fasting the body is cured of its plagues, and by prayer, the mind." Perfect holiness means being purified from both things: *Let us cleanse ourselves from all defilement of the flesh and of the spirit, perfecting sanctification* (2 Cor. 7:1).

Again, there is a certain kind of demon which attacks by spiritual vices, and another kind which attacks by both sorts of vices, namely carnal and spiritual, and this latter kind being stronger *is not cast out but by prayer and fasting*, as is written (Mt. 17:21). It is probable that this sort of demon cannot be resisted either except by these very things, namely prayer and fasting. Therefore, prayer is to be joined to fasting, so that every kind of demon may be the more stoutly resisted.

Again, there are many fasts that are not accepted by God. *Why have we fasted, and thou hast not regarded?* (Is. 58:3). We must labour to make the fasts holy, so that they may be accepted: *Sanctify a fast* (Jl. 1:14). Now it is likely that a fast is sanctified by prayer, just as food is sanctified by prayer, as it is written (1 Tim. 4:5). And thus prayer is to be joined to fasting, so that the fast being sanctified by prayer may be accepted by God; and this is what the Church asks in the Lenten prayer, saying, *Nostra tibi, quaesumus, Domine, sint accepta ieiunia*, and in many other similar prayers.

David joined prayer to fasting in this way when he said, *I humbled my soul with fasting; and my prayer shall be turned into my bosom* (Ps. 34:13). So did Daniel: *I set my face to the Lord my God, to pray and make supplication with fasting* (Dan. 9:3). So also Esdras: *We fasted, and besought our God for this: and it fell out prosperously unto us* (1 Esd. 8:23). So also the Ninevites: *Let neither men nor beasts, oxen nor sheep, taste any thing*; and then: *And let them cry to the Lord with all their strength* (Jon. 3:7, 8). Thus Josaphat: *He betook himself wholly to pray to the Lord, and he proclaimed a fast* (2 Chron. 20:3). Thus Anna the prophetess: *By fastings and prayer serving night and day* (Lk. 2:37). Thus the Apostles also are said to have fasted from the Ascension to Pentecost. The first chapter of *Acts* tells how at that time they persevered in prayer.

With regard to the Rogation days, note that there are normally three reasons why great men bestow gifts abundantly. One is the greatness of their court. For when princes keep a great court, the greater the court is, the more widely do they spread their largesse. So in the Book of Esther it is said that Assuerus made *a magnificent feast for all the princes and for his servants,* and then: *He bestowed gifts according to princely magnificence* (Est. 2:18). The second reason is some triumphant victory, according to the word that David spoke to those who would have prevented the men who stayed with the baggage from receiving anything of the booty: *You shall not do so, my brethren, with these things, which the Lord hath given us... But equal shall be the portion of him that went down to battle and of him that abode at the baggage* (1 Kings 30:23–24). The last reason is the greatness of the one who asks, according to the word that Solomon spoke to his mother: *Seek what thou willest; for it is not lawful for me to refuse thee any thing* (cf. 3 Kings 2:17).

Now, at our Lord's Ascension, there was a greater court in Heaven than there ever had been before, since previously the angels had been there alone, but now the patriarchs and the prophets were there, and the whole of that blessed captivity which Christ brought thither with Himself.

Again, that feast was the feast of Christ's triumph, who triumphantly ascending above all the heavens, as the Victor of a noble triumph, sits down at the Father's right.

Again, He ascends so that He may pray to the Father for us, beseeching the Father's countenance on our behalf.

How great an occasion there was, then, for God the Father to bestow gifts abundantly on a day where so great a court held festival for so noble a triumph, at the intercession of so great an Advocate!

Therefore, in memory of that day, the Church offers prayers and rogations before the Ascension, hoping that she will gain what she seeks more especially and effectively; and so everyone must pray devoutly at this time.

As for the fourth category, note that the Christian religion, knowing that all things happen by divine providence and that all things are established in the hand of the divine power, has recourse to His piety in its needs, whether for fair weather, or for peace, or for similar things, following the example of the ancients, who *cried to the Lord in their affliction* (Ps. 106: 6, 13,

19, 28). Solomon besought our Lord for such men, asking that He might grant the prayer of those who cried to Him in the Temple in their various needs (3 Kings 8).

This beseeching brings a threefold fruit. For sometimes our Lord helps those who thus cry out to Him, so that they may be able to bear their tribulation; sometimes He frees them; sometimes He turns it to great profit. *He shall cry to me, and I will hear him: I am with him in tribulation*, that is, by helping him, which is the first benefit; *I will deliver him*, which is the second; *and I will glorify him*, which is the third (Ps. 90:15). So, since these fruits are so glorious, one should willingly pray in contingencies of this kind, and especially when the Church institutes public prayer for such causes. For the more who pray, the more readily is the divine mercy moved, since as the authority says, it is impossible that the prayers of a multitude should go unanswered.

Commentary on the Rule of Augustine, c.51.

---

3. Why one should willingly pray in a sacred place

ALTHOUGH PRAYERS MAY BE OFFERED IN every place, according to the Apostle's words, *In every place, lifting up pure hands* (1 Tim. 2:8), yet they are poured forth more fittingly and fruitfully in an oratory. St Augustine intimates this by forbidding anything's being done in the oratory that would prevent such prayers.

The truth of this can be shown in many ways. For it is devoutly believed that our Lord more readily answers the prayers that are made in a place set apart for Him for this purpose. *My eyes shall be open, and my ears attentive to the prayer of him that shall pray in this place* (2 Chron. 7:15).

Again, it is to be believed that the holy angels come especially to so holy a place, which is the house of God. As a demonstration of this, Jacob saw *the angels of God ascending and descending* (Gen. 28:12) in the place called Bethel, that is, the house of God.

[7]

But those who pray have need of the angels, who bring their prayers before God.

Again, it is likely that the demons, who like to hinder prayers, do not dare to come to this holy place as they do to others, on account of the terror that strikes them there. *How terrible is this place!* (Gen. 28:17) — terrible especially for the demons.

Again, every oratory is consecrated in honour of some saint. And it is pious to believe that the holy patron of a church has a special care of what belongs to the place whose patron he is, as earthly princes do of those places under their dominion. This is seen with Blessed James and many other saints, who especially help those who go their oratories. Therefore, since those who are praying have no little need of the saints' help — for they are powerful with God, according to the text: *Turn to some of the saints* (Job 5:1) — it is wise to pray in sacred places more than elsewhere.

Again, in most cases the Body of our Lord and the relics of the saints are to be found in an oratory. Now who will doubt but that these have a very great power to provoke salutary prayers? For if a prince more easily receives those prayers that are made to him in the presence of great men, especially when these are his friends, why should one not hope that the same applies to our Lord? So it is said that manna, which foreshadowed our Lord's body, and the rod of Aaron and Moses's tablets, which were, so to say, their relics, were contained in the propitiatory, or the ark (Heb. 9:4), and nowhere else, showing that these were things suited to prayer and propitiation.

Again, an oratory will often have images of the Crucified One, and of the Blessed Virgin, and of the saints and angels. These things bring into our mind the thought of those whom they present to our senses, and such thoughts often have great power to stir up our devotion. But devout love more than anything else make prayer efficacious. Augustine in his letter to Proba about prayer says, "The more affective is the prayer, the more effective it will be", according to the words of 1 Cor. 4:5: *God looks upon the affection of the heart.*[2]

2 Not a literal quotation; cf. also 1 Kings 16:7.

From all this it is clear that the secret prayers should by preference be offered in the oratory rather than elsewhere. This is how that fine man of prayer David acted, saying, *I will worship at thy holy temple* (Ps. 5:8). So also the good and the bad used to do: *Two men went up into the temple to pray: the one a Pharisee, and the other a publican* (Lk. 18:10). So also did the great apostles: *Peter and John went up into the temple at the ninth hour of prayer* (Acts. 3:1).

Commentary on the Rule of Augustine, c.54.

---

4. On the holiness that must be found in prayer: From what it derives, and its effect

ON THE THIRD POINT, NOTE THAT SPIRITUAL men must have three things in particular in their prayers. First of all, the intention of the mind, according to the words of 1 Cor. 14:15: *I will pray with the spirit.* Augustine insisted on this point, when he said: "When you pray to God in psalms and hymns, let what is brought forth with the lips be turned over in the heart."

Secondly, frequency or assiduity, according to the words of Rom. 12:12: *Be constant in prayer.* And Augustine also insisted on this, saying: "Devote yourselves to the prayers".

Thirdly, holy purity, following the example of Job, who said in Jb. 16:17: *When I offered pure prayers to God.* For sanctity is the same thing as purity. And Augustine insists on this when he says of the prayers: "Inasmuch as you frequently hold them, so must you certainly hold them to be the more holy."

Know, then, that in order to have holiness in prayer, one must take heed that the praying tongue be not infected by sin. Jerome says: "I know not what can be going on in a man who prays to God with the same tongue that he uses for lying or cursing or slandering. God pays heed to holy lips, and He quickly grants the prayers that an immaculate tongue recites."

Again, one must take heed lest the hands raised in prayer be stained by some impurity. 1 Tim. 2:8: *I will that men pray in every place, lifting up pure hands.* And afterwards: *In like manner women also (1 Tim. 2:9).*

Again, one must take heed that no pride be evident anywhere in the body, since on account of pride, our Lord does not grant prayers, as is said in Job 35; rather, humility should be evident, by the striking of the breast, by genuflections, and so on, since *the prayer of him that humbleth himself, shall pierce the clouds,* as is said in Ecclus. 35:21. Bernard says: "When hands strike the breast and knees strike the floor, when altars are piled high with vows and devoted prayers, when cheeks are stained with tears and dormitories echo with groans and sighs, and in place of all external business, the holy house resounds with spiritual chant, there is no sight more welcome to the citizens of heaven, no display more gratifying to the most high King."

Again, one must beware lest flitting thoughts gather up within the rational, thinking power, for these *dying flies spoil the sweetness of the ointment* (Eccles. 10:1).

Again, one must beware lest there be in the concupiscible power some desire which is less good. For this stains prayer and obstructs it. Jas. 4:3: *You ask, and receive not; because you ask amiss: that you may consume it on your concupiscences.*

Again, one must beware lest in the irascible power there be any disturbance about another person. 1 Tim. 2:8: *Lifting up pure hands,* that is, in prayer, *without anger or contention.*

Moreover, not only must care be taken lest prayer be stained by such vices, but prayer must also breathe forth every virtue, both theological and political. Thus, prayer must be fragrant with faith, so that our requests may be made in faith.

Likewise, confident hope must be there, so that the one praying does not doubt.

Likewise, charity, which moves one to holy desires, which our Lord will grant more willingly.

Again prudence, so that not harmful things be sought, but helpful ones.

Again, perseverance, which is a part of courage, in order that one may persevere in knocking.

Again, abstinence, which is a part of temperance. For this is a characteristic of holy men, that they join fasting to their prayers.

Finally, the Holy Ghost Himself, the giver of all gifts and virtues, must be found there, causing the prayer to be made with groans inexpressible.

Hence, holiness in prayer arises by avoiding the vices mentioned and from the fullness of the virtues. This is why it is said in Apoc. 5 that the four animals and the twenty-four elders, signifying all the saints, have golden vials, full of odours which are the prayers of the saints; vials, because they lack all stain, which was the first point, and odours, that is of the virtues, which was the second.

Furthermore, this holiness imparts great efficacy to the prayers of the saints, just as malice is a hindrance to the prayers of the wicked. Thus Solomon says in Prov. 15:29: *The Lord will hear the prayers of the just.* Contrariwise, there is a curse upon sinners, since it says in Ps. 108:7: *May his prayer be turned to sin.* And again, Ps. 33:16–17: *The eyes of the Lord are upon the just: and his ears unto their prayers. But the countenance of the Lord,* that is, His anger, *is against them that do evil things.* And Jn. 9:31: *We know that God doth not hear sinners: but if a man be a server of God, and doth his will, him he heareth.* Hence it is that by the prayers of holy Abraham, childlessness was taken away from the house of Abimelech. Gen. 20:17: *When Abraham prayed, God healed Abimelech and his wife, and his handmaids, and they bore children.*

Again, Israel defeated its enemies at the prayers of holy Moses. Ex. 17:11: *And when Moses lifted up his hands, Israel overcame.*

Again, at the prayers of holy Aaron, the scourge of fire ceased. Num. 16:48: *And standing between the dead and the living, he prayed for the people, and the scourge ceased.*

Again, at the prayers of holy Job, our Lord was appeased for his friends. Job. 42:10: *The Lord was turned at the penance of Job, when he prayed for his friends.*

Again, at the prayers of holy Elias, the rain was taken away and later on restored. Jas. 5:17–18: *Elias prayed with prayer that it might not rain upon the earth, and it rained not for three years and six months. And he prayed again: and the heaven gave rain, and the earth brought forth her fruit.*

Again, because of what St Stephen prayed in Acts 7:60, where it is written, *Falling on his knees, he cried with a loud voice, saying: Lord, lay not this sin to their charge,* the conversion of Paul took place afterwards, as the holy doctors say.

From all of these and from countless other examples it is plain how powerful holy prayers are with God. This is not strange, since they delight Him like perfumes. Apoc. 8:4: *The smoke of the incense of the prayers of the saints ascended up before God from the hand of the angel.* Chrysostom says: "Just as finely ground incense pleases those who smell it, so is the prayer of a just man pleasant to God."

From this it is plain in what consists the holiness of prayers, and how powerful they are. And therefore the holy man rightly says: "Inasmuch as you frequently hold them, so must you certainly hold them as holier"; lest, that is, by praying frequently and yet missing the effect of prayer because of a lack of holiness, you should be spending your time in vain.

Commentary on the Rule of Augustine, c.165.

---

5. On giving thanks for good things

THERE ARE SOME PEOPLE WHO ARE FOOL-ishly elated when they see themselves doing what they ought, like those philosophers who *have not glorified God, or given thanks, but became vain in their thoughts,* as Rom. 1:21 says. Against this is 1 Cor. 4:7: *What hast thou that thou hast not received?*

There are others who are not only foolishly elated within themselves, but who also vaunt themselves over others who fail to do what they do, like the hypocritical Pharisee who said in Lk. 18:11: *O Lord[3], I give thee thanks that I am not as the rest of*

3   Douay: "O God".

men. Against this is Rom. 11:18: *Boast not against the branches,* that is, those that were broken off.

There are others who know that whatever good they do is God's gift, but who, from a kind of dullness of mind, do not give Him thanks. Rather, despite receiving His benefits constantly, they remain ungrateful. Against this is Col. 3:15: *Be ye thankful*.

And three evils result from such ingratitude. The first is being deprived of the good that one has received. For as Chrysostom says, thanksgiving is a kind of tax which our Lord levies upon whatever goods He bestows; and so, just as one who does not pay his property tax may be legally deprived of the property on which it was due, so is it with the ungrateful man and the good things he has received. And Augustine says: "That which God had given freely He took away from the ungrateful."

The second evil resulting from ingratitude is that it hinders future benefits. For it is neither usual nor reasonable that a man who is ungrateful for what he has already received should be granted other things. Bernard says: "Whoever gives no thanks for what has been given is unworthy to receive what might be given."

The third evil is punishment, even in this life. For our Lord is not content only to take away from the ungrateful what He had given them, and to bestow nothing else, but sometimes He also adds some temporal penalty. And so Josephus says that after the defeat of Sennacherib, when 185,000 soldiers were slain, although Hezekiah offered sacrifices to our Lord, he did not compose a new canticle of thanksgiving worthy of God, as his fathers had done in similar circumstances, and for this reason, he became sick unto death, our Lord punishing him in this way.

By contrary, three good things result from thanksgiving.

The first is the preservation of those goods which have already been received. Bernard: "Beloved, this is a constant source of sorrow for me, and of sadness in my heart, that I see many prone to facetiousness, to laughter, to chatting, to messing about, and so I am in great fear lest in their excessive ingratitude for the countless gifts of God's mercy, they might be forsaken by grace, which they do not recognise as grace." And so, in the opposite sense, it may be hoped that gifts may be preserved by grace in those who are grateful. For it belongs to our good Lord to conserve in a man those things which that man acknowledges that he holds from Him, and on which he pays the tax that is due. And in this case, the tax is thanksgiving, as has been said.

The second benefit of thanksgiving is the multiplication of good things. For just as ingratitude prevents this, in accordance with Bernard, who says: "Ingratitude is a scorching wind that dries up the spring of love, the dew of mercy, and the waters of grace", so conversely those who give thanks for benefits received are worthy to receive more abundant ones in the present life. And so Bernard says: "From the place whence they came, the rivers of graces return", that is, by thanksgiving, "so that they may flow again."

The third benefit is that one obtains greater things in the next life. For our Lord wills that a man should gain all the profit of the benefits which He confers on him, and that He Himself should receive glory for them. Therefore, whoever does not glorify Him by thanksgiving is worthy of a severe punishment, like an untrustworthy servant who holds on to what is his master's; but whoever does glorify Him will be advanced to greater things in the future, as happens to a faithful servant. Matt. 25:23: *Well done, good and faithful servant; I will place thee over many things.*

Therefore, since so many evils result from ingratitude, and so many good things from thanksgiving, the Church invites us to give thanks, saying daily: *Dignum et iustum est, aequum et salutare, nos tibi semper et ubique gratias agere, Domine sancte, etc.* And Augustine issues the same invitation, saying: "What better can we keep in our minds or utter with our lips or write with our quills, than: 'Thanks be to God?' Nothing more succinct can be said, nothing more welcome can be heard, nothing greater can be thought, nothing can be more profitably given." And Bernard issues the same invitation, saying: "Teach yourself not to be slow or lazy about giving thanks; learn to give thanks for each individual gift." And so, since acting well is a special gift of God, for we can do no good without Him; and since it is very useful, for without it there is no salvation, this holy man rightly says: "When you find that you are doing the things which are written, give thanks to our Lord, who is the one who bestows all good things."

Commentary on the Rule of Augustine, c.205.

---

6. How rancour makes prayer less effective[4]

THERE ARE THREE THINGS THAT PARTICU-larly hinder prayer from having its effect.

The first is the awareness of some serious sin. For if someone has such a sin, and is not penitent for it, how, when he betakes himself to prayer, will he obtain anything from our Lord, bringing before His eyes that which most greatly offends them? And so the psalmist says in Ps. 65:18: *If I have looked at iniquity in my heart, the Lord will not hear me.*

The second thing is unmercifulness. For our Lord customarily conducts Himself toward a man, as that man does toward his fellow. So, when a man does not heed the poor who cry out to him, it is right that he himself should not be heeded by our Lord. Prov. 21:13: *He that stoppeth his ear against the cry of the poor, shall also cry himself and shall not be heard.*

The third thing is cruelty toward another. Is. 1:15: *When you multiply prayer, I will not hear: for your hands are full of blood.* The reason for this is that the wronged man often calls down evil upon the offender, and since he cries out in bitterness to our Lord, our Lord hears his voice more readily than that of the offender when he prays. Ecclus. 34:24: *When one prayeth, and another curseth: whose voice will God hear?*

But rancour, or deliberately cherished anger, contains all three things. For there is no sin that a man can see in his heart so well as this kind of anger.

---

4 In later Latin, the word 'rancor, -is' can be understood as a grudge or bitterness that one retains. Humbert understands it similarly as anger that one holds onto and keeps in existence, translated above as "deliberately cherished anger."

Again, *anger hath no mercy,* as Solomon says in Prov. 27:4.

Again, whoever hates his brother is a murderer, and this because of the cruelty of spirit that he bears. Therefore, since any one of these things is in itself an obstacle to prayer, how much of an obstacle must deliberately cherished anger be, since it includes all three! So it is said in Ecclus. 28:3: *Man to man reserveth anger,* that is, he still has it in his heart, *and doth he seek remedy of God?* This relates to the first obstacle to prayer. It goes on: *He hath no mercy on a man like himself, and doth he entreat for his own sins?* This relates to the second. Then: *He that is but flesh, nourisheth anger, and doth he ask forgiveness of God?* This relates to the third. Therefore, the Holy Ghost says through the mouth of the wise man in Ecclus. 28:2 to whoever wishes to obtain mercy by his prayer: *Forgive thy neighbour if he hath hurt thee: and then shall thy sins be forgiven to thee when thou prayest.* The Son also says in Mk. 11:25: *When you shall stand to pray, forgive, if you have aught against any man; that your Father also, who is in heaven, may forgive you your sin.* And it is said to the Father in Matt. 6:12: *Forgive us our debts, as we also forgive our debtors,* in the hope that the Father will thereby be moved to mercy.

Therefore, by the witness of the whole Trinity it is shown that inward rancour prevents prayer from obtaining mercy. And so Augustine in his Rule rightly says: "They must forgive each other's debts, on account of your prayers", lest on account of rancour those who pray may not be heard, because they are unworthy. As Gregory says, everyone will obtain what he seeks by prayer, when once his mind is no longer darkened by hatred for an enemy.

Commentary on the Rule of Augustine, c.164.

II

On Meditation

1. The subjects of meditation

I T IS PRAISEWORTHY FOR HOLY MEN TO PRAC-
tice meditation. Now, some meditations are about God, insofar as this is possible for a weak intelligence. Thus, from meditation on His justice, a feeling of fear arises; from meditation
on His mercy comes the feeling of hope; from meditation on
His wisdom, seeing all things, comes the feeling of shame; from
meditation on His beneficence arises a holy hunger; and many
other good things arise in the course of our meditation when
we meditate upon God. He meditated in this way who said in
Ps. 62:6: *Upon my bed I will meditate upon thee in the morning*;
that is, "As soon as I awake, I will sit upon my bed, and begin
to meditate on Thee."

Other meditations concern the works of God's creation, in
which many countless things are to be found for us to admire
and to be edified by, and which prompt us to good deeds. Ps.
76:12: *I will meditate on all thy words: and will be employed in
thy inventions*, that is to say, constantly.

Other meditations have to do with the words of re-creation,
which are great and wonderful and full of saving acts. Ps. 118:117:
I will meditate always on thy justifications; that is, on the works
of re-creation by which we are justified.

Others, again, concern the pains and martyrdom of the
only-begotten Son of God, which He endured in order to create
us anew. These should be numbered and weighed, and always
kept in one's memory. Ps. 118:24, 99: *Thy testimonies are my
meditation*. This martyrdom is called 'testimonies', because tes-
timony is the same thing as martyrdom, or because His passion
testifies to us of His charity, love, and similar things.

Other meditations are of God's deep judgements: how He rejects some people in anger, but is appeased in regard to others, and so on. Ps. 76:7f: *I meditated in the night with my own heart*; that is, not with flesh, for I had not fleshly meditations but spiritual ones. He explains what they were, saying: *Will God then cast off for ever?* etc.

There are others which pertain to the divine law and its study. Ps. 118:97 *O how have I loved thy law, O Lord! It is my meditation all the day.* It is as if he were to say; "Other people love other subjects, and so spend some time studying those; but I love Thy law so much that I spend the whole day studying it and meditating upon it." In fact, the just man studies it not only during the day, but also at night, and so *on his law he shall meditate day and night.*

Others are about the commandments of God, that we may see what should be fulfilled and what should be omitted, what done and what avoided. Ps. 118:15: *I shall meditate on thy commandments*; that is, by listing them and pondering over them, to see in what I have transgressed, and to what extent I have been at fault, and which things should have been done, and which avoided.

Other meditations concern the divine words, which are full of power and much edification. Deut. 11:19 *Teach your children, that they meditate on them*, namely, on My words. Those who wish to build themselves up do this by taking some word, and seeing what power and edification they can draw from it.

Other meditations refer to one's own evils and feelings, and also other people's evils and the wretchedness of this world; and this causes one to sigh. Is. 59: *They seem to meditate, and to sigh in meditating.*[5]

Others refer to the reparation that must be made for evils committed. Ecclus. 14:22: *Blessed is the man that shall continue in wisdom, and shall meditate in his justice*; that is, he shall meditate on how he may do justice here concerning his past sins, before a heavier justice is done to him hereafter.

Other meditations are of future evils, which induce fear, in order that fearful things may not come upon us. Is. 33:18: *Thy*

5   This does not occur in Is. 59.

heart shall meditate fear; that is, it will meditate on those things which strike fear into one, such as the pains of hell, the day of judgement, purgatory, death, the judgements of God, and similar things.

Other meditations refer to good things to be done, so that what is commanded may not be neglected. Prov. 15:28: *The mind of the just studieth wisdom*; and another version has "studieth obedience"[6]. That is, he thinks about the obedience whereby he omits none of those things that he is obliged to do from the commandments of God, or from some other cause.

Other meditations refer to one's duties of state. For this is something which everyone ought to think about carefully and in good time. Hence, in the *Lives of the Fathers*, it is said that a certain elder, whenever he had to begin some task, always stood still beforehand for a long time, meditating. 1 Tim. 4:15: *Meditate upon these things*; and he is speaking of the things that were incumbent on him because of the office and grace that he had received.

Other meditations refer to what one has to say. For every good man must be especially on guard not to speak without first thinking. And as he thinks, he must make sure to say nothing but the truth. Prov. 8:7: *My mouth shall meditate truth*.

Again, he must make sure to say nothing but what is good and holy. Ps. 34:28: *My tongue shall meditate thy justice*; that is, just and holy things.

Again, he must take care to speak only with wisdom even what is true and holy. Ps. 36:30: *The mouth of the just shall meditate wisdom*.

Again, he must take care that what he says may be either to the praise of God, in accordance with Ps. 34:28, *Thy praise all the day long*, that is, "this is what my tongue will meditate", or else for the upbuilding of one's neighbour, in accordance with Ps. 48:4: *The meditation of my heart* will speak *prudence*[7]; the gloss says: "About behaviour".

6   Douay has this latter.
7   Douay has "understanding".

And note that in these passages the tongue or mouth is said to meditate, and meditation is said to speak, because in a holy man, meditation always brings it about that he does not say anything except what is true and good, and that also in a wise manner, and to the praise of God or the benefit of his neighbor; and so meditation causes the just man to speak.

---

2. *The value of meditation*

KNOW ALSO THAT HOLY MEDITATIONS OF this kind benefit greatly the one who meditates. First of all, they stir up his spirit. Ps. 76:7: *I meditated in the night with my own heart: and I was exercised,* that is, by meditating. Now the exercising of the spirit is of much greater value than the exercising of the body, for this latter avails only a little.

Again, such meditations purify the soul. Hence, the same psalm continues: *And I swept my spirit,* that is, by meditations.

Again, they enflame the heart. And so, Ps. 38:4[8] says: *In my meditation a fire shall flame out.*

Again, they subjugate the flesh. Eccles. 12:12: *Much study is an affliction of the flesh.*

Again, they help in countless ways to bring about a well-ordered life. In his book, *On Consideration,* which means much the same as 'Meditation', Bernard says this: "Consideration first of all purifies the mind in which it arises. It then governs the feelings, directs actions, corrects excesses, controls our behaviour, makes our life worthy and orderly, resolves doubts, strengthens what is slack, gathers together what is scattered, scrutinises what is hidden, investigates the truth, tests what is plausible, determines what is false and illusory, plans our actions, and thinks over what we have done, in order that there may remain nothing in the mind which is either uncorrected or in need of correction. It is consideration that foresees trouble in peaceful times, but which heeds not the troubles when they come, thus showing both

8 Not Ps. 76, as the text implies.

prudence and courage. Consideration sits like a judge between necessity and pleasure, and decides on the bounds to be fixed for each, giving to the former what is sufficient for it, and taking from the latter whatever it has in excess, and in this way it gives to them both a third virtue, which people call temperance. As for justice, it is clear that consideration comes to the mind first, so that the mind may shape itself according to this very virtue. For the mind needs first to take thought in such a way that from itself it may declare the requirements of justice, intending neither to do to others what it would not want done to itself, nor to deny to others what it would have done to itself."

So from all this it is clear what subjects good men should meditate upon, and how useful this kind of devotion is.

Commentary on the CONSTITUTIONS, c.30.

III

Of Secret Prayers

1. In commendation of secret or freely chosen prayers

WE SHOULD OBSERVE THAT THE FACT OF Augustine's forbidding hindrances to those who might want to pray in the oratory outside the fixed times is a clear commendation of secret prayers. Prayers like this are an evident token of holiness, and should be practised by religious men with all diligence. Our Saviour left us an example of this, for although He needed nothing, He is often recorded as having prayed, that He might encourage us by His example to do the same. The Apostles also left us an example of this, saying when they left the ministry of tables for this purpose: *Look ye out among you...whom we may appoint over this business. But we will give ourselves continually to prayer* (Acts 6:3–4). Nearly all the old saints have left us an example of this, as is obvious from their lives. Thus the holy father Paul the first hermit was discovered after his death propped up against a tree, with his hands and face turned toward heaven, as it were praying. A special example of this has been left to us by our holy father St Dominic, who very often spent the whole night in prayer, having no bed. And those who saw the early days of the Order say that the first brethren also left us an example of this. So when one of the early brethren, who is supposed to have gone simple from too much devotion, came to Paris, and one day entered our present church there and found no friar praying in it, he recalled how the original little church that used to be there had nearly always been full of brethren praying in it, and he asked who the church belonged to which is there now, and being told that it belonged to the brethren, he said, "Impossible! This is not a church of the Friars Preachers. Their church is a little one, full of brethren kneeling in prayer before all the altars throughout the church. This one is nothing like that." From which it is clear how assiduous the brethren were in such prayers at that time.

To appreciate the value of these prayers, one needs to know that they have certain advantages over the solemn prayers which are said by rule at the fixed times and seasons in the ecclesiastical office. For the prayers that are found in the common office are for the most part acts of praise rather than requests. Now praises are especially suited to the homeland, where is enjoyed all that which was sought by petition, according to those words: *In that day you shall not ask me any thing* (Jn. 16:23). On the other hand, petitions particularly belong to the way thither, which is a state of being in need, according to the words, *Ask,* which refers to prayers, *and you shall receive* (Jn. 16:24) glory, which refers to the divine praises. Now secret prayers are petitions more than praises, and so they are more necessary in the present life.

Moreover, in the common office, when petitions are made, these are for specific things, and sometimes they are for things of which someone present may not be in much need. But in the secret prayers, each one seeks what he desires according to his own needs, in the way that Augustine says in his prayer: "I am wretched, Thou art merciful; I am weak, Thou art my physician", and so on. And everyone needs to labour more for that of which he has greater need.

Moreover, the prayers of the common office come from the Church's institution, whereas the secret prayers are of divine institution, according to the words: *But thou...having shut the door, pray to thy Father* (Matt. 6:6). And our Lord is recorded to have given us an example of praying in this way, but not in the other way. So, they are of greater necessity, which is why they pertain to everyone.

From these three things it is clear that secret prayers are more necessary than the other kind.

Again, they have something in them which seems to make them more powerful. For they are more mental than vocal, which does much for the efficacy of prayer. *When I invoked,* that it, spoke with *in*ward *voice*, God heard me (Ps. 4:2).

Moreover, they beget a greater love. For the one who prays in this way can delay more on each petition as he meditates, and from this lingering way of thinking are generated more movements of holy desire. Such movements of love make prayers much more powerful, according to the text: *Thy ear hath heard the desire of their heart* (Ps. 9:38).

Moreover, they are purer. For nothing vain can be mingled with them, as easily happens with vocal prayers, which are performed before men. But the purer a prayer is, the more powerful it is. Bernard says in the commentary on the *Canticle of Canticles*, "How pure and sincere is the prayer of one who has no regard for praises, untempted by flattery!"

So from these three things it is clear that these prayers are more efficacious than others.

Again, they are poured forth more gladly, according to the words: *In his sight I pour out my prayer* (Ps. 141:3). But the prayers poured forth in the sight of men are not poured forth so gladly, since they are sometimes hindered by them.

Moreover, they can be offered more spontaneously. For whereas common prayers may require particular books, as well as companions and a suitable place and a fixed time, these do not, but can be prayed at every time and place and with no companions. Thus it is said in Ps. 41:9: *With me prayer to the God of my life*, as if to say, "It is in my power".

Moreover, even when the strength of the human body fails, the spirit must not fail. So it is written of St Martin when he was sick, "Unconquered, he did not relax his spirit from prayer." This does not apply to the divine office.

From these three things it is clear that it is easier to pray in this way.

Therefore, since these prayers are more necessary than others, and more powerful in many respects, and easier to offer, it is clear that they have many advantages over ordinary prayers. For this reason they must be practised with all devotion.

Commentary on the Rule of Augustine, c.53.

2. *Of the time and place of secret prayer*

A NYONE WHO WISHES TO PRAY IN THIS WAY, that is, to pray with much devotion, must choose a time and a place. Bernard says in his commentary on the Canticle of Canticles, "Whilst every place is suitable for this kind of prayer, a hidden place is more suitable and a sacred place best of all."

With regard to praying in any place at all we have the Apostle's words: "I will therefore that men pray in every place, lifting up pure hands" (1 Tim. 2:8). For this reason, the brethren pray not only in sacred places but also in those that are not sacred. They pray not only in the convent, but everywhere: now in guest-houses, now on the road, now in the cell, now at table, now after the meal, now on their beds, now in passage-ways, now in the schools, now as they read their books, now in the garden, now in the cloister. They pray everywhere, whatever the place may be.

With regard to praying in hidden places we have what Isidore says in his work *De Summo Bono*: "Prayer is more appropriately offered in private places". So it is that our Lord, who is God, set an example of this by leaving the noisy city and going to a desert place where there was calm. There He prayed, hidden from sight (Mk. 1:35).

As for praying in a sacred place we have these words: "My house shall be called a house of prayer" (Matt. 21:13). This shows how suitable for praying in is a place dedicated to God, since this is what gives it its name. In fact, what was said above about the suitability of a church as the location for the divine office applies to these prayers also. This is why Augustine lays down in his Rule that nothing else should be done there, so that those who wish to pray there outside the canonical hours may not be prevented. This is also why devout men are accustomed to visit sacred places gladly, and in the morning before they begin their day's work or as they are beginning it, to go to a church to pray. Our Saviour used to do just this. When He entered the city, He was accustomed first to visit the temple or a synagogue, thereby giving an example for us to do likewise. To the verses that show how when He entered Jerusalem He first entered the Temple (Matt. 21:12), the gloss adds: "Thus giving the pattern of religion; so that wheresoever we go, we may first enter the house of prayer, if there is one, and having commended ourselves to God, then return to our own affairs." And it is from here that the custom arose for religious who return to the cloister to visit the oratory first. Likewise, those who are religiously minded do the same when they enter villages or cities or towns, if they conveniently may.

Now, although these prayers may be offered at any time, the better times are those specially set aside for them, and the best of all are the morning and the evening. With regard to praying at any and every time, we have St Luke: *We ought to pray always, and not to faint* (Lk. 18:1). So it is that holy men pray, so to speak, continuously: now at the start of their works, now in the middle, now at the end; now in good fortune, now in bad; now on account of the evils they undergo, now for the good things they lack. Sometimes they pray for the goods they desire now, sometimes for those they wish to have in the future. They pray now for themselves, now for others; now for the living, now for the dead; now for those in high estate, now for the lowly. Sometimes they pray for those who travel amidst great dangers. They pray for those who are dear to them, and for their enemies; for their benefactors and their malefactors, and so on throughout all the numberless needs that are forever cropping up in this our poor old world.

As for praying at fixed times, we have Augustine's words: *Devote yourselves to the prayers at the appointed hours and seasons.* He means by this, certain fixed times of the day and also certain seasons of the year, such as the Rogation days, and many other similar times. This is *to pray without ceasing*, namely, when someone never passes through a time appointed for prayer without praying, as the gloss explains on this very verse (1 Thess. 5:17). For we believe that not without good reason were certain times and seasons and feast-days and similar things especially set aside for prayer. So, devout men pray more and with greater devotion at these times, as being times where prayer is offered more seasonably. *Every one that is holy shall pray to thee in a seasonable time* (Ps. 31:6).

As for the very best times to pray, we have Bernard's observation in the commentary on the Canticles, "Free time is more convenient for prayer and more suited to it." Time is called free when it is empty of employment. This is true especially of the morning, before we tackle our daily work, and of the evening, when we lay aside our employments. This is why these two times are particularly set aside by us for prayer, that is to say in the morning after matins and lauds, and in the evening after compline. At these two times the brethren must always give themselves to the secret prayers, whether they are in the priory or outside it, though more or less according to the time of year.

These are the two times that David, that excellent man of prayer, kept in his own devotions. He kept the morning-watch, for he says: *In the morning my prayer shall anticipate thee* (Ps. 87:14); and he kept the evening, where he says: *The lifting up of my hands as an evening sacrifice.*

Christ did the same, to induce us to follow His example. He prayed in secret in the early morning, for it is said: *Rising very early, going out, he went into a desert place: and there he prayed* (Mk. 1:35). And He prayed in secret when it was late, according to the text, *He went into a mountain alone to pray. And when it was evening, he was there alone* (Mt. 14:23).

These are the two sacrifices of the law, not carnal but spiritual, namely the morning and the evening one, which we are commanded to offer each day (Ex. 29).

We must pray early and late, so that by offering both the beginnings and ends of our actions to Him who is Alpha and Omega, the first and the last, we may pay to Him what we owe — the first fruits which are the beginnings of our actions and the tithes which are their completion. We must pray early so that we may be directed by prayer in our daily actions, as the final prayer of prime itself requests. We must pray late, so that we may be fortified by prayer against the temptations of the night; and the final prayer of compline asks for this. These prayers do not change, as the final prayers of the other hours do according to the season, because we always have these unchanging reasons to pray at these two times, whereas at other times we may vary something in the object of our prayer.

What is more, these two times are suited not only for prayer but also for meditation. The early morning is well-suited to meditation because the soul is then more clear and can see more deeply. This is why David used to meditate at this time, saying: *To thee do I watch at break of day* (Ps. 62:2). The even-tide is also suited for meditation, since the human spirit is then recollected from its activities, and has turned back to itself. So it is said to one who was busy during the day: *When thou hast acquitted thyself of all thy charge, take thy place* (Ecclus. 32:2), that is, "having time then for thyself".

This also agrees with the judgement of philosophers. Jerome says in *Against Jovinian*, "These are Pythagoras's precepts: take care of two times in particular, namely the early morning and the evening; that is, of the things that you are about to do and those that you have done." This is as much as to say, these are the times for meditation.

A holy man gives time in the early morning both to meditation and to prayer. Thus it is written: *The just man will give his heart to resort early,* by meditation, *to the Lord who made him, and he will pray in the sight of the most High* (Ecclus. 39:6). Time should also be given to both prayer and meditation in the evening. Therefore, at the start of the evening office of compline comes the versicle, *Converte nos, Deus, salutaris noster,* that is to say: "Convert us from outward things to inward ones, so that we may be able to give time to Thee", which pertains to meditation; and then comes the response, *Et averte iram tuam a nobis,* as if to say, "In case that we have offended against Thee in anything this day"; and this is a prayer.

From all this it is clear how assiduously and for what reason we should fervently practise the devotion of secret prayers.

Commentary on the Constitutions, c.32.

IV

On The Manner of
Instructing Novices

1. Concerning prayer

I N REGARD TO PRAYER, THE MASTER OF NOV-
ices must not only instruct them about the psalms, and about
how to say the set prayers; he must also teach them how to make
devout supplication, now for the remission or avoidance of sin
or various offences, now for the removal of certain defects, now
for the gift of certain graces and virtues.

Again, he must teach them that in their prayer they are to
aim to stir up contrition and compunction, rather than to make
long speeches.

Again, he must teach them to be mindful not only of themselves, but also of their relations and friends and acquaintances
and benefactors, and even of persecutors and of unbelievers who
do not know God, and of others who are still far away from God,
entangled in various sins.

Again, let him teach them to spend their spare time in prayer
of some kind, and to choose some suitable place for this in the
church: they can either go round all the altars there, making
some special prayer before each one, or they can say their prayers
in some other part of the church.

Again, he should teach them to trust more to common prayers
than to their individual ones. They should be more prompt to
take part in common ones, whether these are the liturgical hours,
or the private prayers said after compline and after matins, taking
great care to say them well and devoutly. He should teach them
not to leave choir without necessity before the end of the office,
or before the end of the thanksgiving after the meal; and even

when these are finished, they should not leave until they have said some further prayers, commending themselves to God.

Again, he should teach them that when they are reading or hearing something read, and they learn thereby how they are guilty of some fault of omission or commission, or how some good things are lacking to them, they are to turn to prayer during the reading, asking to be freed from these evils and to obtain those goods.

Again, he must teach them to have recourse to prayer in time of perplexity and doubt, and in temptations and difficulties, and at the beginning of every new action. He must teach them to accustom themselves to make petitions for the removal or forgiveness of whatever evils they see or hear, and to give thanks for good things, and to praise God always in all things, both favourable and unfavourable.

Again, let him teach them how they must strive to apply their heart to whatever they say in their prayers; and yet, how they should not give up hope of their prayer's bearing fruit if they do not always do this; and how they must not give into the rather fierce attacks which the enemies sometimes make upon them, nor give up their prayers on account of these things.

Again, he should teach them not to lie face down when they pray, or to stretch their arms out in a cross or to let their heads drop down too much; rather, when they pray they should kneel up straight, or inclined just a little.

On Duties, c.5.

2. On meditations

AGAIN, THEY SHOULD BE TAUGHT TO SPEND time in meditation, either when they are on the road, or when they walk up and down in the cloister, or in the garden, or in some other part of the house, or when they are engaged in secret prayers, or when they are at rest in their cell or lying awake upon their bed.

Such meditations should be made sometimes about the general gifts of God, and sometimes about His more particular gifts; sometimes about the giving of thanks, and the ingratitude of the human race; now about the works of creation, now about those of the redemption, such as the incarnation, and the passion, and so on; sometimes about the rewards of the good, and sometimes about the punishments of the wicked. Sometimes they should meditate upon punishments that have already been meted out, and sometimes upon mercies that have already been shown; they should meditate now about creatures, now about the Scriptures; now about their own defects, and now about the progress that they have made. Let them meditate sometimes upon the tricks of devils, and sometimes about the services of the angels; sometimes about the examples of the saints, and sometimes about the perversities of the perverse. They should meditate now about their inner state, now about their outer state; sometimes thinking again over what they have done, and sometimes thinking about what they are to do; meditating now about the omnipotence of God, now about His knowledge, now about His goodness, now about His strictness, now about His mercy, and now about His justice. Let them meditate sometimes on His manifest judgements, and sometimes on His hidden ones.

Different emotions should be elicited by means of these and similar meditations: now hope, now fear, now sorrow, now groaning over evils, now sighing after goods, now wonder, now exclamation, now thanksgiving, now petition, now shame, now reverence, and so on. All these things are learned more by experience than by teaching.

On Duties, c.5.

---

3. How they should behave in choir

IN CHOIR, LET THEM ALWAYS BEHAVE RELIGIOUSLY and in a sensible way, with recollection, and without laughing or letting their eyes wander. They must be always well disciplined, so as not to offend anyone who sees them, and especially, both then and at other times, when in the presence of the brethren and of secular persons.

Again, they are to say the canonical hours and the office of our Lady and the office of the dead without haste, devoutly and clearly. Each verse must be finished before going on to the next, and they must allow the verse of their companions with whom they recite the office, whether in choir or outside, to be finished before they begin their own. The next verse may never be begun before the previous one has come completely to its close.

Again, novices should have a most particular devotion to the Blessed Virgin Mary, honouring her and serving her in every other kind of way. They should think of her as the very devoted and beloved mistress and protectress and abbess of their Order, and they should place in her a special hope and trust, as their greatest refuge after God.

Let them also carefully note that serving Mass is the special duty of novices, and let them do this very gladly and with all devotion. For there is present there the source of all goodness and mercy: the God-man who sits at table and casts a morsel of bread to a puppy. For He who is rich in mercy will not disdain to grant at least a crumb of grace and devotion to a novice who serves devoutly and carefully at the Lord's table. For our generous Lord, who is rich toward all, is not so discourteous to the novice who thinks of himself as like a dog, that is, something lowly and abject, but that He will grant to him something when he devoutly asks.

And let novices also note this, that many novices, by willingly and devoutly serving at Mass, have surpassed others not only in the religious life, but also in learning. For there they draw that which afterwards they pour forth with devotion.

On the Instruction of Novices[9], c.5

---

9 This particular work was written by Jean de Montlhéry, OP, a thirteenth-century Parisian Dominican and contemporary of Humbert of Romans.

PART II

The Divine Office

I

The Hours & the Psalms

1. Which and how many are the canonical hours, and why prayers are more especially to be offered at these times

I F IT BE INQUIRED WHICH ARE THOSE APPOINTED times and seasons mentioned in the Rule, the answer is that the appointed times are those canonical hours which, according to ancient usage and also according to the custom of those religious who have preserved this usage, are eight in number, namely matins, lauds, and the other six hours of the day. For according to this custom, lauds are said separately from matins at the start of dawn.

And thus God is praised eight times in the natural day by the Church under the New Covenant, just as He was praised eight times under the Old Covenant, as is found in Nehemiah 9:3, although the ways of dividing the hours are different.[10] Blessed Benedict lays down this distinction of the hours in his Rule in imitation of that fine man of prayer, the prophet David, who says: *I rose at midnight to give praise to thee* (Ps. 118:62), which refers to the first matins, and again: *Seven times a day I have given praise to thee* (Ps. 118:164), which refers to the other seven hours, the first of which is lauds, which, according to this custom,

---

10 Neh. 9:3 says: *They read in the book of the law of the Lord their God, four times in the day, and four times they confessed, and adored the Lord their God.*

is said as the day begins. This hour of lauds is clearly different from matins, since it has its own opening, with the words, *Deus in adiutorium nostrum intende*, and its own hymn, as the other hours do. But the common modern practice is to say matins and lauds together, which are then counted as one hour, since they are concluded by a single prayer. In this way the canonical hours are brought down to seven, which is a more sacral number. The Davidic saying: *Seven times a day I have given praise to thee*, is then taken to refer to the whole natural day, with one time of praise at night, and six in the day-time which follows that night, namely prime, terce, sext, none, the prayer of the eleventh hour which is vespers, and that of the twelfth which is compline.

Now if anyone should ask why these hours rather than others have been appointed as the ones at which to pray to or praise God, the answer is that we read that the saints set aside these times in particular for prayer and for the divine praises. So David says, *I rose at midnight to give praise to thee* (Ps. 118:62), which is one hour; and again, *Evening and morning, and at noon I will speak and declare* (Ps. 54:18), which makes three more, namely vespers, prime and sext. The Apostles were praying at the third hour when they received the Holy Ghost. Peter and John used to go to the Temple that they might pray at the ninth hour of prayer (Acts 3:1). And Christ is said to have prayed at around the twelfth hour which is called compline, when after the supper He poured forth His prayer to the Father (Jn. 17).

Again, these hours mark out certain remarkable deeds that pertain to our redemption. For our Saviour was born at night; He arose at the first hour of the day; He sent the Holy Ghost at the third hour; He ascended at the sixth; at the ninth He died on the Cross; at the eleventh, that is at vesper-tide, He gave His body and blood in the sacrament at the Supper; and at the twelfth He was buried. Justly then have these times been set apart for the divine praises and for holy prayers more than other hours, at which no such deeds are recorded to have happened.

Again, we read that the father of the family sent out the labourers early in the morning, which is prime, and likewise at the third hour, at the sixth, at the ninth, and at the eleventh which is vespers, and called them to their reward at the twelfth hour, compline. So since the divine office is called 'the work of God', rightly do these hours belong to the divine office. Nor is it unfitting that to these six hours of the day is added a divine work at night, for the work of the contemplative life pertains not only to the day but also to the night, for which reason Jacob is said at night to have wrestled with the angel (Gen. 32:24–32). Expounding this passage, Gregory says that this wrestling is contemplation.

In fact, these three explanations of why these hours have been assigned to the divine office are also reasons to pray more fervently at these times; for we should pray all the more gladly at those hours when the saints are said to have prayed, being privileged hours; at hours that mark out the works of the Redemption, so that we may have a share in them; and at the hours assigned to God's labourers.

Commentary on the Rule of Augustine, c.46.

---

2. *Why we use the psalter in the office more than other books*

THE CHURCH USES NO PART OF SCRIPTURE in the office so much as the psalms. There are many reasons for this. First, it is right that those who gather for the divine office should remember David, who from being so great a sinner came by repentance to a rank of such greatness as a prophet that everywhere on earth his prophecy is preferred to all others in the divine praises. In this way, those who come to office are strengthened in our Lord, trusting in His kindness, if they are willing to do penance.

Again, no part of Scripture is so spiritual as the psalms: for just about every verse speaks of God, especially those which are more frequently encountered in the divine hours. And so with God being as it were thus placed before the eyes, the mind is greatly lifted up to what is above.

Again, this part of Scripture produces countless salutary effects. A certain author, said to be Augustine, gives a full account of these as follows: "The singing of psalms puts to flight the demons, it causes holiness, it refreshes the mind, it enlightens like the sun, it flows like oil, it extinguishes unlawful desires, it checks wrath, it penetrates all things, fills all things, it deifies man, it opens his understanding, it bestows the desire of the Kingdom of Heaven, enkindles a spiritual fire in the heart, expels the roots of all evils; it is a consolation in sorrow, a knowledge of the true light, and it removes weariness from the soul; whoever loves the perpetual singing of psalms cannot commit sin." And many other things are mentioned in the same work.

Again, this part of Scripture is more common than others; that is, everything which is said in it applies in general both to the just and to the impious, into one of which two categories all men fall.

Again, this is the part of Scripture that contains all that is needful for human instruction. A gloss in the preface to the psalter says: "In this book is the summation of all theological learning". For the rewards of good men and the punishments of wicked men are described in it, as are the first steps of beginners, the progress of the proficient, the life of active men and the meditations of contemplative ones. In this book is related what sin takes away, what penance restores, what the penitent says who is aware of sin, and what he acquires through his repentance.

Again, this part of Scripture excels the others, especially the prophets, in clarity, as is said in the same gloss on the psalter that was mentioned above. For others speak in enigmas, but this one speaks more clearly, and for the most part without figures.

Again, there is hardly anything in the psalter but what is either the praise of God, or petition: the two things which especially pertain to the divine office.

Again, because of the way the verses are set out, the psalms are so composed as to be more suited to vocal praise than the other parts of Scripture, and this is something necessary for the divine office. Hence, David himself used to sing them before the ark; and as Isidore says in the *Etymologies*: "It is called the psalter, because one prophet used to sing with his psaltery, and the choir would reply in unison."

Again, the word 'psalm' comes from 'psallere', which means 'to touch'. For it is a form of divine praise which was done not only by means of the voice, but also with an instrument, with the hands acting in accordance with the voice. This signifies that, when it comes to the praise of God, actions should accompany words, as a gloss says on the verse in Ps. 146:1: *Praise ye the Lord, because a psalm is good.*

We may gather from all this why the singing of psalms is suited to the divine office: it strengthens us in God, raises minds to what is on high and leaves behind in them a great number of salutary effects; it contains things which are relevant to all people, teaches all things necessary, is clearly understood, is composed of the things that befit the divine office, is suited to vocal song, and by its very name teaches us the worthy manner of praising the Creator. This is why the Church uses the psalms more than the other scriptures in the divine office.

And so, since the office consists for these good reasons mostly in psalmody, great care must be taken that no disorders arise when the psalms are sung.

Commentary on the CONSTITUTIONS, *c.33.*

---

3. Of the Lord's prayer, and why this more than anything else is most properly called prayer

THERE ARE THREE PRAYERS WHICH THE Church's custom particularly puts before us: the *Credo in Deum*, which the apostles made; the *Ave Maria*, which the angel made; and the *Pater Noster*, which was made by the Son of God.

Now, among all the Church's prayers, both these and others, the *Pater Noster* enjoys pre-eminence for several reasons. It has, first of all, the pre-eminence of being more properly a prayer than the *Credo in Deum*, the *Ave Maria*, the psalms, and the other things which are said in the Church, since although these are thought of as prayers, for the most part they are not properly speaking prayers, but rather praise, or something of that kind. The *Pater Noster*, however, and everything in it, is truly prayer in the most proper sense of the term.

Again, it has pre-eminence on account of its author, since the inventor of this prayer is incomparably more excellent than the inventors of all other prayers.

Again, it has pre-eminence from its completeness, since it contains everything needful to mankind, as has often been explained by the learned, which is not true of any other prayer.

Again, it is pre-eminently easy. It is short, and so is easy to learn. Hence, no one can be excused for not learning it and having it by heart, or for getting bored with it and failing to say it often.

Again, it is pre-eminent in virtue of its commonness; that is, nothing in it is sought for a private person, but everything is sought for all in common. And it belongs to charity to prefer what is common to what is private.

Again, it is pre-eminent because of the certitude that it carries with it of being pleasing to God. For in regard to other prayers, we do not know whether they will please God; but who can doubt that the prayer which He Himself has taught us to say will be acceptable to Him?

Again, it is pre-eminent in regard to its effect. As Augustine says, it blots out daily faults, something which is not said of any other prayer. Therefore, since the Lord's prayer is so powerful, it is good for it to be used very often in the Church's office, just as costly spice is mixed in with vegetables of lesser price when making a sauce, so that the sauce will be better.

Now, those who have a shorter office ought to mix in this prayer more often, so that its power will make up for what is lacking in the quantity of the office. Therefore, it was right that we who have a short office ought not only to say the Lord's prayer in the *preces*, as many churches do, but also more often, and so we say it before and after each hour of the office.

At the end of each hour, when we always say the Lord's prayer, this is especially for the faithful departed. We thus make up, in a sense, for the fact that we say the office of the dead less frequently than many others do.

We say the Lord's prayer before each hour of the divine office for two reasons. One is so that by the power of the Lord's prayer, we may be granted to say the office in a way worthy of the divine praise, which is difficult. The other reason is that by the merit of the office which is about to be said, we may gain that which we ask for first of all in the Lord's prayer.

Commentary on the CONSTITUTIONS, c.43.

II

Of those Hours of the Office which should especially be attended

1. Why one should rise very willingly for matins

ALTHOUGH WE MUST BE DEVOTED TO THE divine office at all times, for three of the hours there are particular reasons why we should attend the divine office more especially. These are matins, prime and compline. This is contrary to the practice of those who hardly ever get up for matins, and almost always find bogus pretexts to stay away, as if going to the divine praises in the day-time alone were enough for them.

These men do not seem to belong to that blessed and innumerable throng standing before the throne of God, of whom it is said that not only in the day but rather *day and night they serve him in his temple* (Apoc. 7:15).

These men are not of those holy living creatures who not only do not rest in the day but who *rested not day and night, saying: Holy, holy, holy, Lord God Almighty, who was, and who is, and who is to come* (Apoc. 4:8).

They are not of those guardians of Holy Church, who not only during the day but *all the day, and all the night shall not hold their peace* (Is. 62:6), that is, shall not fail to praise the name of our Lord. Such a man is roused by the prophet Jeremias, who said, *Arise*, that is, rise with others [con*surge*], *give praise in the night* (Lam. 2:19).

David was not prevented either by his royal business during the day or by the charms of his wives during the night from rising very promptly for the divine praises at night, as it is written, *I rose at midnight to give praise to thee* (Ps. 118:62).

[40]

Christ sometimes spent not just a part of the night but the whole night in prayer: *He passed the whole night in the prayer of God* (Lk. 6:12).

Paul and Silas were not prevented by the constraints of their prison from rising in the middle of the night and praising God. *At midnight, Paul and Silas praying, praised God. And they that were in prison heard them* (Acts 16:25).

Unhappy are those sleepy ones who are not roused by such and so great examples to get up at night for matins!

Moreover, women too rise at night to take care of their house. *She hath risen in the night, and given a prey to her household, and victuals to her maidens* (Prov. 31:15).

Again, workmen stay up for a good part of the night to make money. *So every craftsman and workmaster that laboureth night and day* (Ecclus. 38:28).

Again, those who are zealous for wisdom rise at night earlier than workmen. According to Jerome, "Demosthenes says that he outdid all workmen by his vigils."

So, if those who are zealous to acquire wisdom rise at night, as well as workmen seeking gain and women taking care of their houses, how much more must the servant of God rise at night for the service of the eternal King! This is why Paul says: *In all things let us exhibit ourselves as the ministers of God*, and adds, *in watchings* (2 Cor. 6:4), intimating that the man who shirks the sacred vigils is no true minister of God.

Next, the night-time is more suited to the acts of the contemplative life, since it is quieter, and more free from occupation. And so it is said: *In the daytime the Lord hath commanded his mercy*, that is, the works of the active life, *and a canticle to him in the night* (Ps. 41:9), which pertains to the contemplative life.

Again, blessing is due to God not only in the day but also in the night, according to the text, *O ye nights and days, bless the Lord* (Dan. 3:71).

Again, the enemy of the Church attacks not only in the day but also at night. Bernard says: "He will neither slumber nor sleep who attacks Israel". He can be resisted by the sacred vigils.

When the sun was set, Jonathan commanded his men to watch (1 Mach. 12:27), that is, on account of the enemies whom he had heard were to come up at night.

Again, temptations of the flesh often accompany those who are sleeping, which is why Paul mentions them together, saying, *Not in chambering and in impurities* (Rom. 13:13). Honourable vigils repress these things, according to the text, *Watching for worthy things consumeth the flesh* (Ecclus. 31:1).

Moreover, to get up for matins is very punishing, which is why Paul enumerates vigils amongst his labours, saying, *In much watchings* (2 Cor. 11:27). Therefore, it has a greater satisfactory value.

Again, just as our Lord came to Balaam at night (Num. 22), so He more frequently visits the soul in this time of silence, and infuses inner consolations. *He hath given songs in the night* (Jb. 35:10), that is, joyful consolations.

Therefore, we should rise willingly for matins, lest we lose the time most apt for prayer; so that we may fully render the debt of blessing to God; so that we may aid the Church when she is attacked; so that we may escape the temptations of the flesh; so that we may gain the merit of satisfaction for ourselves; so that we may gain a share in holy consolations, and so that we may provide for bodily health in the service of God. And the prophetic word bids us do this: *In the nights lift up your hands to the holy places, and bless ye the Lord.*

Commentary on the Rule of Augustine, c.47.

---

2. Why one should rise willingly in the morning for divine office

THERE ARE SOME, AGAIN, WHO BEING HELD fast by the pleasantness of morning sleep hardly rise early enough for prime, that is, for morning prayer, not rising *iam lucis orto sidere*[11]. Against these stands the Apostle's word: *It is now the hour for us to rise from sleep.* And he gives the reason,

11 "When the sun is up" (the first line of the hymn for prime).

saying: *The night is passed, the day is at hand* (Rom. 13:11, 12).

Note also that wickedness causes people to get up early. *He riseth at the very break of day* (Jb. 24:14), that is, the murderer rises with his accomplices.

Human necessity also makes people get up early. *The sun ariseth*, and then, *Man shall go forth to his work* (Ps. 103:22, 23).

Again, Nature also does this. Thus the birds begin to sing very early in the morning, shaming man a-lazing in his bed. So Ambrose says in the *De officiis*, "What Christian will not be ashamed to pass through the day without psalmody, when the smallest birds anticipate the sun and the dawning of the day with their devotion?"

Therefore, if wickedness, necessity and Nature awaken others for their various tasks, how much more should charity rouse us up early in our Creator's service!

Thus Job rose early not only for himself, but also for his sons. *Rising up early he offered holocausts for every one of them. And so did Job all days* (Job 1:5). So acted David, who stirred up not himself alone but even his instruments of music that they might rise early with him for the divine praises: *Arise, psaltery and harp: I will arise early. I will give praise to thee* (Ps. 56:9–10). Thus did Isaias, who said: *With my spirit within me in the morning early I will watch to thee* (Is. 26:9). Thus did Christ Himself go early to the common place of prayer: *Early in the morning he came into the temple* (Jn. 8:2). Sometimes He went to a secret place of prayer: *Rising very early, going out, he went into a desert place: and there he prayed* (Mk. 1:35). So, finally, does every just man: *He will give his heart to resort early to the Lord that made him, and he will pray in the sight of the Most High* (Ecclus. 39:6).

One should note that an early morning vigil leads prayer to be more quickly answered. There are two witnesses to this. The first is Baldad the Suhite: *If thou wilt arise early to God, and wilt beseech the Almighty*, etc., and it follows, *He will presently awake unto thee* (Jb. 8:5, 6). The other witness is David, saying: *For to thee will I pray: O Lord, in the morning thou shalt hear my voice* (Ps. 5:4).

[43]

Again, such prayer often receives the sweetness of divine consolation; thus the manna, which signifies Christ, was gathered in the morning (Ex. 16:21); and it is said, *They that in the morning early watch for me, shall find me* (Prov. 8:17).

Again, it is said: *In the morning you shall see his glory* (Ex. 16:7), and: *The third day was come, and the morning appeared*, and then the Law was given (Ex. 19:16). What is sweeter than to find our Lord, to see His glory and to hear Him giving the commandments of life? All of this, according to these authorities, is granted to the one who keeps vigil early. For just as a man is more easily found at his home in the morning, so is God found in the heart. Then also the soul, having a greater clarity, is better able to contemplate the glory of God, on account of which the Psalmist says: *In the morning I will stand before thee, and will see* (Ps. 5:5). Then also she as it were hears the Teacher, who gives His lesson early and instructs souls. *In the morning he wakeneth my ear, that I may hear him as a master* (Is. 50:4).

It is in such vigils that the devil is frequently confounded, along with his host, the vices. *Now the morning watch was come, and behold the Lord looking upon the Egyptian army, slew their host* (Ex. 14:24). Alas! To how many then sleeping does it happen to the contrary: the devil rushing upon them, slays them, just as enemy forces sometimes overwhelm a camp early in the morning when the men are sleeping!

How fruitful, then, is the morning vigil, in which prayers are more swiftly heard, divine consolations more frequently received, and enemies more triumphantly cast down.

This time of day is more suited, also, to raising one's heart to God, before the soul is drawn down by its diverse occupations, or hindered by the images it has picked up. That is why it is said of the just man, *He will give his heart to resort early* (Ecclus. 39:6), as it were having then more power over his heart.

Moreover, there is then a greater need of having recourse to God, so that He may direct us in the activities and contingencies of the day, just as David did, when he said: *In the morning my prayer shall prevent thee* (Ps. 87:14).

Therefore, we must rise willingly for our Lord in the early morning for the divine office, on account of the benefits that have already been mentioned, because of the appropriateness of the hour, and because of our needs. And thus it is said in Wisdom 16:28: *We ought to prevent the sun for thy blessing*, that is, to bless Thee, *and adore thee at the dawning of the light*.

Commentary on the Rule of Augustine, c.48.

---

3. Why one should come willingly to compline

THERE ARE OTHERS, AGAIN, WHO AVOID COM-pline, whereas religious brethren should on the contrary take care with great diligence never to miss this office, on many accounts.

For it is clear, first of all, that this hour is the one where one passes from active labour to contemplative rest, which is why we chant the words: *Nunc dimittis, servum tuum, Domine, secundum verbum tuum in pace.* Now it belongs to good minds to make this transition willingly, and not to prolong the activities of the active life beyond the daytime, according to the words, *Man*, who uses reason, *shall go forth to his work*, that is to his activity, *until the evening* (Ps. 103:23), and not beyond.

Again, since there is *a time to keep silence and a time to speak* (Eccles. 3:7), this is the hour in which silence begins for religious, to which all good religious must come to more willingly than to conversation. Augustine: "Let there be speech for necessity and silence for delight".

Again, this is the hour at which the holy living creatures who go to outward things during the day return to things within,[12] and so at the beginning of this office it is said: *Converte nos, Deus, salutaris noster*, that is, convert us from outward things to inner ones. Now this is very characteristic of a good mind.

Again, according to our custom, secret prayers are joined to compline, and those who do not come lose the benefit of these.

12 Apparently an allusion to Ez. 1, but not a direct quotation.

Against this it is said: *Thou when thou shalt pray, enter into thy chamber*, that is, into the secret place of thy heart, *and having shut the door, pray to thy Father in secret: and thy Father who seeth in secret will repay thee* (Mt. 6:5). And Bernard says in his commentary on the Canticle of Canticles, "How calm and pleasing is prayer when no noise disturbs it!"

Again, many things are done in this hour, and not at others, by which a certain grace is conferred, such as the sprinkling with holy water and *the blessing of the father*, that is, of the superior, which *establisheth the houses of the children* (Ecclus. 3:11).

Again, those who frequently stay away from compline use their time worse than those who stay away from the other offices of the day. For those who stay away from the other offices will often be giving themselves to hearing confessions or to study or to some other fruitful work; but those who stay away from this office give themselves to useless talking or to some carnal amusement. But how greatly must everyone beware lest that time which is spent in a holy fashion by others is spent badly by himself! *Son, conserve the time* (Ecclus. 4:23), that is, keep it with others, that you may spend it well just as they do.

Again, those who keep away often disturb the others by staying up and making a noise and coming into the dormitory late — all things of which one must beware in regard to the servants of God. For the one who disturbs them grieves the Spirit of God dwelling within them. For Gregory says in the *Dialogues*: "When a holy man is stirred to anger, who else is provoked to anger if not the One who dwells within him?"

Again, they do not only disturb others but also give scandal to them. For when they see them staying away from compline, they will not easily find a reason to suppose that they stay away except for an insufficient motive, and so they are scandalized in them. But if *it were better for him that scandalizes one of these little ones that a millstone should be hanged about his neck* (Mt. 18:6), what shall we think of him who scandalizes one whole convent?

Again, we commend ourselves solemnly to the Blessed Virgin at compline. Now it is certain that such a solemn act of commendation is very efficacious, which is why Master Jordan related what he heard from a certain religious man, that when the brethren said: *Eia ergo advocata nostra*, he used to see the Blessed Virgin on bended knees, commending the Order to her Son.

How foolish, then, is he who does not gladly make himself present for such a commendation!

Therefore, let the holy brethren gladly come for compline, for the love of contemplation, for the love of silence, for their care for their own conscience, for the benefit of the secret prayers, to obtain other graces, from care not to spend their time uselessly, so that the brethren may suffer neither disruption nor scandal, and from devotion to the glorious Virgin.

What wonder is it if spiritual men gladly seek repose as the day declines, since even birds then cease their chattering and take rest? And Pliny says that at that hour, the whole swarm of bees within the hive, hearing one of their number fly around it, fall silent and rest until morning, when hearing the same bee fly around again, they are stirred up and once more arise.[13]

Commentary on the Rule of Augustine, c.49

---

4. Why one should willing hear Mass

THERE ARE MANY MOTIVES WHICH SHOULD induce all the faithful, but especially religious, to hear Mass every day. For it is certain that while there are many other kinds of sacrifice, such as prayer, praise, and so forth, yet none of them has such power as the sacrifice of the altar. For it is particularly offered *pro circumstantibus*, that is, for those who are at hand. Indeed, it is offered for all who are dear to them, as is clear from the words of the Canon.

Again, at Mass, refreshment is administered to souls, and bread to sustain that life which daily flags.

Again, the brazen serpent is raised there for the eyes of faith, set up on a pole to heal the venomous wounds that are daily inflicted.

13 The last paragraph is not included in Fr Hering's selection.

Again, the theological virtues are exercised at Mass, so that they may increase and gain merit. How much faith merits there, since its glory lies in believing what is not seen! There is scarcely any other point of faith which brings so much merit. Hope is raised up at Mass, as it trusts in the One at whose table it sits. And there is charity supremely enkindled, mindful of that love which was shown us on the Cross.

What reason could there be to neglect so powerful a Victim, offered for oneself and for all one's own, in every manifold need; to neglect a food so necessary for man, man who is constantly prone to collapse; to neglect a remedy that saves us from the dangerous wounds that daily pierce us; or to neglect so great an aid to virtue and to merit, while we still have the possibility to advance?

Moreover, the angels come daily to attend Mass, as the Fathers say, though they do not need such helps, and although this sacrament was not instituted for them, simply out of reverence toward it. How much more should man be daily present, for whose benefit it has been established!

Again, what contempt it shows that a man on earth neglects to go to a place nearby where he can find the King of heaven who has come thither on his account.

Again, what sense does it make to ask daily for one's daily bread, if when such an excellent bread is sent from heaven, it is slighted by the one who asked?

For this reason, it is customary to oblige those who have missed Mass through negligence to go to as many Masses as they missed.

Commentary on the CONSTITUTIONS, c.25.

III

On the Manner of Reciting the Divine Office

1. Of those things that are necessary for reciting the Psalms with devotion

WITH REGARD TO DEVOTION IN RECITING THE divine office, note that there are some who are undevout or not very devout when they say the office. For some say it simply from habit, without thinking of the meaning. Others do attend to what they are saying, but they are not affected by it. Others are affected with some feelings, but not with joy, which is very necessary in this form of service. Others, again, have joy, but lack the seriousness which takes away frivolity. Some have both joy and seriousness, but may along with these things have pride and so they look down on others; while others who have along with these things humility instead, yet sometimes do what they do without freedom of spirit, and as if out of necessity, like slaves and not free men.

Now, devotion is a fervent will to do something, manifested by evident signs. Therefore, in order that the divine office may be recited with devotion, it must be said not just from habit, but with understanding, with feeling, with joy, in a mature manner, humbly, freely. Bernard says in his commentary on the *Canticle of Canticles*: "When we immolate the sacrifice of praise, let us take every care to unite understanding to habit, feeling to understanding, gladness to feeling, seriousness to gladness, humility to seriousness, and freedom to humility." Devotion of this kind fattens the sacrificial victim and makes it a holocaust full of marrow; it is such holocausts that we must offer, and not scrawny ones. Ps. 65:15: *I will offer up to thee holocausts full of marrow.*

Commentary on the CONSTITUTIONS, *c.28*

Again, note that to sing psalms worthily to the heavenly king, three things are needful: the intention of the heart, a reverent posture, and disciplined chant.

The intention of the heart means that everything which is brought forth by the lips should be turned over in the heart.

The posture must be reverent so that in the divine praises the very body should assist reverently.

The chant must be disciplined, so that in the very singing itself due discipline is preserved.

On the first point, the Apostle says in Eph. 5:19: *Singing in your hearts to the Lord.* This is what he did himself, for in 1 Cor. 14:15 he says: *I will pray with the spirit*: that is, turning over in my spirit that which I pray; and *I will pray also with the understanding*; that is, I shall not allow any useless thoughts into my understanding at that time.

But not only useless thoughts must be driven forth at that time; even necessary ones must be, if they relate to temporal concerns; in fact, even thoughts which at the proper time are salutary, such as thoughts about the Scriptures and so on, must be excluded, as Bernard says in his work on the Canticle of Canticles. And he adds: "The Holy Ghost will not accept and welcome anything which you offer Him at that time other than that which you owe, if you have neglected what you owe". Hence, we must sing psalms, and sing them wisely, as Ps. 46:7–8 says. A gloss says: "No one does wisely that which he does not understand." This is not surprising, since wisdom proceeds from the heart; how then will something be done wisely which is done half-heartedly?

On the second point, Bernard says in the same commentary: "When you take your place to sing psalms, hold yourselves reverently." Truly, the brother who sings psalms in church must stand with reverence; for the place in which he stands is holy. The altars, crosses, images and relics among which he stands are things of great worth; so is the array of brethren, who are also to be honoured; the angels too stand around, in whose sight he sings; and the One before whom he stands looks on, in His supreme majesty. All these demand reverence.

Therefore, let the brother reflect on the holiness of the place in which he stands, the worth of the things among which he stands, the community of the brethren with whom he stands, the presence of the angels in whose sight he stands, the excellence of the supreme majesty before which he stands; and let him stand with reverence for the divine office in choir. Let him avoid what happens to some, who keep the hood of their white capuce over their head and let their black one slip down, or who are dishevelled in some other way. Let him not cross his feet or sit with legs akimbo, or show his shins unfittingly, or let his limbs be in any other way undisciplined. Let him not clear his throat noisily or scratch himself unpleasantly, annoying other people with these or other bad habits. His eyes should not rove about but be cast down, and he should stand before the great majesty not with a bold face, but with modest eyes. He should not fidget, moving now here now there, now leaning on one elbow, now on the other. He should manifest the stability of his mind by the stability of his body, never giving way to any kind of silliness, but displaying maturity at all times. He must not break the silence, nor offend God by any other transgression, nor disturb those who are with him by any faults. He must make the accustomed bows and prostrations reverently in the proper way, omitting none.

With regard to the third point, the discipline of the chant, note that some, who come to sing praise from compulsion, bring a kind of sadness along with them, and so their music is less acceptable, since music and mourning do not go well together, nor do songs befit a sad person.[14] The opposite should be done, for one should sing psalms with such gladness that it will be outwardly apparent. Ps. 94:2: *Let us make a joyful noise to him with psalms.* A joyful noise means gladness manifesting itself outwardly.

There are others, again, who articulate the psalms in a lazy and languid way. They do this not from religious gravity, but because they are lackadaisical. And yet it is said to everyone in Ecclus. 31:27: *In all thy words be quick,* that is, not lazy.

---

14 The reference 'Eccl. 22' is inserted here, but these words are not to be found in this chapter of Ecclesiasticus.

Now, if idle men are not worthy to stand before earthly kings and perform any service, as one may gather from the words of Prov. 22:29: *Hast thou seen a man swift in his work? He shall stand before kings*; how much less may such men stand before the King of heaven! Therefore, in order that those who sing the psalmody in a lazy manner may be roused, it is often said in the psalms, "Sing psalms to our God, sing psalms to our king, sing psalms!", just as a lazy donkey is often pricked and is told: "Go on, go on, go on!" to overcome its laziness.

There are others who are sleepy and careless during the psalms. Bernard says in the work, *On the bad monk*: "He is vigilant about tales, sleepy about vigils." Against this it is said in Ps. 32:3: *Sing well unto him with a loud noise*. For someone does a thing well if he does it vigilantly; and to sing with a loud noise is not done by those who are sleepy, but by those who are awake. Therefore, whoever is wide awake and diligent about the psalmody sings well with a loud noise.

There are others, again, who seem to be feverish. They continually stretch themselves, and yawn, filling their mouth with air, when it ought to be full of a psalm, according to the words of Ps. 70:8: *Let my mouth be filled with praise*. Bernard says of the bad monk: "He is a great drinker, but a feeble singer." Against this, it is said of David when he sang psalms before the ark of the covenant in 1 Par. 13:8: *David played before the Lord with all his might, with hymns, and with harps, and with psalteries*. Someone who sings psalms with all his might does not pretend to be weak.

There are some who so fear to tire themselves out by making a lot of noise, that they sing very quietly so as hardly to be heard by those singing with them. Against this, the psalmist says in Ps. 9:3: *I will sing to thy name, most high*. Take 'most high' here as an adverb.

Again, there are some who skate over the words of the psalms so quickly, or come in so abruptly, that they scarce pay what is due. Against this, the psalmist says in Ps. 60:9: *So will I sing a psalm to thy name, that I may pay my vows*.

There are others again who sing the psalms with such weak and feeble voices that they seem more like women than like men. Against these, it is said in Ps. 97:6: *Sing praise to the Lord with long trumpets, and sound of cornet.* These instruments have a strong sound, not a weak one.

From all this, it is clear that to sing in a disciplined manner, as is proper, the psalmody must be done with joy; lazy spirits must be aroused, sleepiness shaken off; one must not pretend to be weak, nor be apprehensive that it will be burdensome when this is not the case; everything must be well articulated, and the singing must be virile. And so David is called an *excellent psalmist* in 2 Kings 23:1, since, as is clear from what has been said, he taught by word or example that all this must be done in the psalmody. Blessed Bernard also taught his sons to sing the psalms like this, saying in a sermon on the Canticle of Canticles: "I admonish you, beloved, that when you take part in the divine praises, you come willingly before our Lord; do not be lazy, do not be sleepy, do not yawn, do not spare your voices, do not clip off the ends of the words, do not miss out entire words, do not have weak and feeble voices which will make you sound womanish, but rather bring out the words always with a virile dedication and devotion, as is fitting."

So, that makes clear what three things are necessary for psalmody to be praiseworthy.

Commentary on the CONSTITUTIONS, c.28, 34.

---

2. With what heart one should pray

WHEN THE HEART SUFFERS FROM WANDERing in prayer, this happens sometimes from human weakness, sometimes from negligence, and sometimes from deliberate choice. While all of these are bad, the third is worse than the second and the second worse than the first.

Some thoughts are about necessary matters, as when someone has something to do and needs to think about it, of which it is said, *The earthly habitation presseth down the mind that museth upon many things* (Wis. 9:15).

Some thoughts are of vain things: *The Lord knoweth the thoughts of men, that they are vain* (Ps. 93:11).

Others are of iniquitous things: *Perverse thoughts separate the soul from God* (Wis. 1:3).

In prayer, one must beware of the first kind of thoughts, but more of the second, and still more of the third.

Again, some thoughts arise from the suggestion of demons. Others come from a preceding fault, as when before prayer someone so lets his mind wander, that as a result things come to him, as if he were dreaming, which hinder his prayer. Others come from a present fault, as when someone is occupied in something else when saying his office. The first is bad, the second worse, the third worst of all.

Again, in prayer, thoughts sometimes crop up which are useful and are related to the prayer, as when by reason of a certain word in a prayer, one thinks of something that will be useful for a sermon. Sometimes the thoughts are useful, but unrelated to the prayer. Sometimes they are both unrelated to the prayer and useless, or rather harmful. The first kind have some excuse, the second have less, and third have least of all.

According to these foregoing distinctions, one may decide to what extent someone who suffers from the wandering of his thoughts as he prays need fear for his conscience.

If now it is asked whether someone who does not think about what he is saying is bound to repeat the canonical hours, one can reply that the wandering could be so great, and so blameworthy according to the principles given above, that he would be so bound. Otherwise he is not; it is enough for him to confess it. The judgement of these things is left to reason and to the anointing.[15] Or it can be said that when one has said the hours

---

15 The reference to 'anointing' here should be understood as a reference to the aid given by the Holy Spirit, beginning in Baptism and strengthened with Confirmation. Thus, the judgment should be made by reason and the aid of grace.

with one's lips, one is never bound to repeat them, since the obligation pertains only to the outer act.[16]

Yet all must strive, and especially religious, that when they pray, *what is brought forth with the lips may be turned over in the heart*. Otherwise their prayer will be apish. For apes sometimes move their lips as if they were praying. *This people honoureth me with their lips* (Matt. 15:8).

Again, when it comes to teaching or to debating or to craftsmanship or to any kind of activity, including bodily ones, a man is reckoned foolish who does not think about what he is doing or making. So on the text: *Sing ye wisely* (Ps. 46:8), the gloss says, "No one does wisely what he is not thinking about". How much more does this apply to prayer! *The mouth of wise men is in their heart* (Ecclus. 21:29). This is said because what they say, they also turn over in their heart.

Again, when someone speaks to his neighbour he thinks about what he is saying, and all the more so, the more important is the one to whom he is speaking. Therefore, since in praying we speak to the most high God, a man must be most sure to think as he prays. Bernard: "When you enter the church to pray, leave outside the din of your fluctuating thoughts, so that you may be with God alone." For it is not possible that someone should speak to God whilst he is chattering to the whole world, even though he may be in silence.

Again, prayer is the heart's food. So just as someone loses the savour of some good piece of food when he does not chew it, so one loses the savour of spiritual prayers by not grinding the prayer with the teeth of one's intelligence. Bernard says: "Food is savoured in the mouth, psalmody in the heart." Let the soul not fail to grind it with the teeth of the understanding, lest having swallowed it whole, its palate will miss that savour which is more delightful than honey and the honeycomb.

Again, we are seeking in our prayers that God might be attentive to us, according to the text: *Be attentive to me and hear me* (Ps. 54:3). Now how likely is it that He will do this, if we are

16   This paragraph does not appear in Hering.

not attentive to ourselves? Bernard: "How shall He be attentive to me, who am not attentive to myself?"

Again, it is from the heart that prayer takes most of its power. Augustine says: "His ears are rather to the voice of the heart than to that of the body." And Isidore: "Prayer is of the heart, not of the lips." For God does not attend to the words of the one beseeching Him, but He looks rather on the heart of the man who prays. So the man who does not have his heart in his prayer takes away from prayer what is best in it.

So it is clear from all this that the heart's intention is necessary in prayer. Thus the prophet David said in 2 Kings 7:27:[17] *Thy servant has found his heart, that he may pray to thee.* And the Apostle says, *I will pray with the spirit, I will pray also with the understanding* (1 Cor. 14:15). And of the just man in general it is said: *He will give his heart to resort early* etc., and then: *And he will pray in the sight of the Most High* (Ecclus. 39:9). And Peter encourages us to do this, saying: *Watch in prayers* (1 Pet. 4:7). The gloss adds, "Let the mind not think of anything other than the prayer it is making."

So that this may be more easily done, the heart must be first recollected when one comes to pray.

Sometimes as well one should look at the book, so that the heart may be the better able to apply itself to the things that are said.

For the same reason, some people like to number the verses as they are saying the psalms, or to find similar ways of keeping distractions at bay.

However, it should be known that even when from human weakness someone cannot have his heart firmly in his prayers, he should not for that reason weary of praying, since even though a poor man may not be continuously crying out, he nevertheless moves the master of the house to have pity on him simply by his bodily appeal as he sits there at the gate all day long. And much more should one trust in the mercy of our Lord.

Moreover, the very sound of the prayers, as is devoutly believed, has a great power, like the words that charm snakes.

17 Not chapter 27, as Hering has.

Again, when there was a meritorious intention at the beginning of the prayer, the whole work that follows is meritorious, even if one is not always actually thinking about it, and the work of prayer avails if not as a prayer at least by way of merit.

Commentary on the Rule of Augustine, c.57.

---

3. Of the evils that follow when the office is too long

WE SHOULD NOTE THAT MANY PROBLEMS arise when the divine office is too long.[18]

The first is the emptying of the choir. For many brethren seek reasons and permissions to stay away when the office is too long, and so the choir becomes empty.

The second problem is harm to the brethren. For there are few so strong and healthy in body as not to be sometimes harmed and weakened from an excessive office, and so afterwards those who ought to be in choir have to stay in the infirmary.

The third problem is boredom, which more or less everyone suffers when something continues too long. Now, this is very much to be avoided in the divine praise and the divine office, since we should take part in it, on the contrary, with enthusiasm. Jerome says: "I prefer to sing one psalm with gladness of spirit than the whole psalter with dullness, and weariness, and sadness of soul."

The fourth problem is that the office gets deformed. A long office cannot be said so correctly and worthily as a short one. It is more praiseworthy to say a little well than to say much badly, for people are praised on account of qualities, not of quantities.

---

18 Humbert is apparently warning in this section against singing too slowly. The number of psalms to be sung in any given hour was not a matter of choice. Lest moderns gain a wrong impression from this passage, it may be worth recalling that for the Dominicans, ferial matins contained twelve psalms, while Sundays matins contained eighteen (excluding the invitatory). Lauds included seven psalms and an Old Testament canticle, while vespers contained five psalms. This was the pattern until the reform of Pope Pius X was imposed on the Order in the 1920s.

That is, one deserves more for producing something good than something big; and a craftsman who produces little but does it well is more worthy of praise than one who produces many things, but bad ones.

The fifth problem is that it gets in the way of other good things. Among other good things, we refer here to two of particular importance, namely devotion and study, each of which is inhibited by an excessive office. With regard to devotion, note that there is one kind of devotion which bears on the divine office itself. This is shown when the office is said devoutly in common. The other kind is that to which the brethren are accustomed to give themselves after the office, spending time in meditations and secret prayers. These meditations and secret prayers are called devotions, both because they arise from devotion, that is, from free choice and not from the rules of the Order, and also because from them, generally speaking, devout and holy affections are garnered.

Commentary on the CONSTITUTIONS, c.27.

---

4. *Why the divine office is said solemnly on feast days*

ON FEAST DAYS, THE OFFICE SHOULD BE CARried out in a more solemn way, and the psalms should be sung with greater pauses being made. This is because, on such days, the brethren are not so occupied with lectures or study, and hence the reason for shortening the office, namely the fact that it hinders study, is then largely absent.

Again, on feast days a greater number of outsiders generally come to the office, and it is right that it should be said with greater devotion in order to edify them.

Again, on feast days, they are obliged to give more time to God, since this is why feasts were instituted. Hence, it is fitting that they should spend more time at His office on those days.

Again, the community is normally better fed on those days. For this reason, they should labour more diligently in the service of God, who provides for them, just as a faithful labourer works more diligently at his master's work when he is better provided for.

Again, the enemy hates feast days, and tries to cause disturbances on them. For this reason, the choir should take greater care to solemnize them with more devotion, lest he should be victorious.

Again, feast days symbolize that great, future feast in which praise will be perpetual and perfectly devout. Hence, so that the sign may correspond better to what it signifies, the office of the divine praise should be performed with all devotion on feast days.

Here, then, are six reasons: the first, from us; the second, from our neighbor; the third, from God's side; the fourth, on account of the reward; the fifth, on account of our adversary; and the sixth, from the very nature of a feast.

Commentary on the CONSTITUTIONS, c.36

---

5. Why the office should rather be said inside the church than outside

ONE SHOULD NOT QUICKLY SEEK REASONS or permissions to stay away from choir. The office should be said more willingly there than outside, for many reasons.

First of all, prayers are granted more readily in a church, because it is a place dedicated to God. So 2 Par. 7:15 says: *My eyes shall be open, and my ears attentive to the prayer of him that shall pray in this place.*

Again, there is a greater number of people there; and a multitude is more able to obtain what it asks for, which is why our Lord says in the gospel, in Matt. 18:19: *If two of you shall consent, concerning anything whatsoever they shall ask, it shall be done to them by my Father.* How much more will this happen when a great multitude asks for the same thing.

Again, the holy angels join those who sing psalms, as Bernard says on the verse of Ps. 67:26: *Princes*, that is, heavenly ones, *went before joined with singers.* Glorious it is to have such companions in psalmody.

Again, in church, the office is done in a more correct way, with no omissions or negligence, since some are appointed who have special care about this. But if the queen of Sheba was so delighted to see the good order of Solomon's ministers, how much more glad must be a soul, devoted to the eternal king, to see an office in which He is served in an ordered and beautiful way, than one where He is served in a less well-ordered manner.

Again, our Lord's body is in the Church, and the relics of the saints. We may well believe that on account of their presence, some special grace is granted to those who venerate them, just as jesters normally carry away some boon from great men when they desport themselves before them. This is why David sang psalms before the ark. And according to 2 Par. 3, two cherubim, who signify clergy and religious, were made by Solomon with their feet aslant, as if ready to exalt, on the side of the ark, which represents the body of our Lord.[19]

Again, the devils fear a church, because of the body of our Lord, the relics, the crosses, the angels, the holy water, and other holy things which are inside it. This is why we sing: *Terribilis est locus iste*, "How terrible is this place", namely, to the demons. For this reason, they are not as able to interfere with those who sing psalms in a church as elsewhere, since they dare less to approach it.

Again, vocal prayer itself produces many useful and holy effects. One is that it makes the heart to melt with holy desire. Hence, it is said of Augustine that he was greatly moved by the hymns and canticles and the sweet song of the Church, and wept abundantly.

Again, it elevates the mind. Bernard says: "The sound of praise lifts up the eyes of the mind." Consequently, many are caught up into an ecstasy during this kind of song. This is why in Ps. 67:27–28, after the verse, *In the churches bless ye God the Lord*, it goes on: *There is Benjamin, a youth, in ecstasy of mind*.

Again, vocal prayer dispels evil sadness. On the verse of Jas. 5:13, *Is any of you sad?*, a gloss says: "Frequent and pleasant psalmody dispels the plague of depression." Again, David says in Ps. 70:23:

19 Not chapter 13, as Hering has. Humbert seems to have a different reading from that of the Clementine Vulgate.

My lips shall greatly rejoice, when I shall sing to thee, that is, "I shall be so filled with joy, that it will appear in my lips".

Again, it prepares a way in the heart for our Lord, so that He may infuse into it many different graces. Gregory in his commentary on Ezekiel says, "When the sound of psalmody is produced from an attentive heart, then a way toward the heart is prepared for our almighty Lord". *Sing a psalm to his name, make a way for him* (Ps. 67:5). And again: *When the minstrel played, the hand of the Lord came upon Eliseus* (4 Kings 3:15).

These are the four beneficial effects of the chant as regards the soul.

Again, it puts the devil to flight. *David took the harp, and played with his hand, and Saul was refreshed, and was better, for the evil spirit departed from him* (1 Kings 16:23).

Again, it delights God; so in the Canticle of Canticles, He says to the Church, *Let thy voice sound in my ears* (Cant. 2:14).

Again, it turns the Church militant into an image of the Church triumphant, which is ever in jubilation. Bernard in his commentary on the Canticle of Canticles says, "Nothing on earth so exactly mirrors any aspect of the heavenly dwelling as eagerness in praising God."

Again, it alarms the enemies of the Church. *And when they began to sing praises, the Lord turned their ambushments upon themselves, and they were slain* (2 Chron. 20:22).

Happy effects are these, and good is that jubilation which melts hardness of heart, raises up the earthly mind, drives away the sadness of this world, prepares a path for the divine blessing, puts the devil to flight, delights God, makes the Church militant like to the triumphant, and puts her enemies to shame!

How willingly, then, is the office to be recited there where the holiness of the place causes prayers to be granted more quickly, and where a multitude more easily obtains what it asks, where heavenly spirits join themselves to mortals to praise the Creator, where the eternal King is served in a more orderly way, where Christ Himself, with the relics of His saints, is present in Person, where wicked spirits are less able to hinder us, and where vocal praise leaves behind so many and such great effects! Hence it is said in Ps. 67:27, *In churches, bless God the Lord.* This is why our Lord, on the day of judgement, will say to those who preferred to stay away from the choral office of matins that which is written in Job 38:7: *Where were you when the morning stars praised me together, and all the sons of God made a joyful melody?* The apostles didn't set us an example of staying away from choir, of whom it is said in Luke 24:53: *They were always in the temple, praising and blessing God.* And this is true of the time before they had dispersed themselves through the world to preach.

Rightly, therefore, has it been laid down that our brethren are to hear the divine office together in the church, unless the superior has dispensed some of them.

Commentary on the CONSTITUTIONS, *c.26.*

---

6. Why the office must be said properly when one is not in choir

ALL SHOULD TAKE CARE THAT THE OFFICE never be said outside choir except in a proper, religious manner. For since the brethren often have to say the office outside choir, and since a very great part of our penance consists in saying the office, those who say the office badly outside choir do a very great part of their penance badly.

Again, when the office is garbled, there can be no devotion of the heart, which is what is most important in the office, and particularly acceptable to God. Therefore, in this way the office is deprived of what is best in it.

Again, it cannot be without offence to the Creator when the office due to His majesty is said improperly. For the Creator must be placated through the office; and what a thing it is, to be provoked to anger by the very office through which He should be appeased!

Again, when care is not taken to say the office properly in these circumstances, a man gradually acquires the habit of saying it badly; and once someone has become accustomed to do this, he can hardly be corrected, as can be seen by many examples.

Again, all those who witness the office being said badly are scandalized, both outsiders and others. And what a thing it is, when those who by their profession are bound to strive for the edification of all scandalize men by their deeds, especially by the very things which relate to God!

Again, this is a fault for which nearly all clergy and countless religious need to be corrected; but how will they correct them, when they themselves suffer from the same fault?

Again, the ecclesiastical office is extremely noble, since to praise God is something angelic. Now eating, drinking, and similar things, which are bestial and ignoble offices, are taken very seriously. So how unworthy it is, when an angelic and very noble office is performed negligently!

Therefore, although the brethren who say the office outside choir are not obliged to observe the same pauses as are made in choir, they must nonetheless recite it in a decent fashion always and everywhere, lest they omit a great part of their penance, deprive the office itself of its value and power, offend the Creator in the very thing wherein they ought to placate Him, fall into an incorrigible vice, scandalize those whom they ought to edify, deprive themselves of the means to correct others for this fault even though this is their proper task, and prefer bestial and ignoble offices to this angelic and most noble one.

Now, in order that the office may be said worthily and in a proper manner outside choir, it must be said integrally, correctly, out loud, clearly, unhurriedly, attentively and reverently.

It must be said integrally, which means that none of those things which have to be said in choir, or which are written down, are left out, neither the office of the dead, nor the proper of the Mass that is due to be said on that day, or at least its introit, nor any commemoration, and so on. The only exception is that the beginning of the antiphon, which is recited in choir so that the psalm may be correctly intoned, does not need to be said before the psalm, since the Church in general does not do this, and since they are not recited before the psalm for the sake of beginning the psalm as such, but in order that the psalms may be sung, which does not apply here.

The office must be said correctly, which means that another prayer should not be used instead of the proper one, or another chapter instead of the proper one, and so on.

It must be said out loud, not between one's teeth, but sufficiently loudly so that it may be heard and understood.

It must be said clearly, so that each word is clearly pronounced, and a new verse is not begun before the previous one has been finished.

It must be said in an unhurried manner, so that one does not race through it and say as much as possible in one breath. It should be sufficiently drawn out that as many breaths may be taken as are needed to pronounce everything. For just as in singing the office one must guard against dragging things out, in reading it one must guard against speed.

It must be said attentively, so that one does not at the same time engage in anything that could distract one from thinking about what is said, as some do by cutting quill-pens, or cutting their nails, or marking their books and so on. The heart should be withdrawn from other things as far as possible, and wholly set upon thinking about the office.

It must be said reverently, with the prostrations being made where this is possible, and always at least some bows, even if not so many as are made in choir, as a sign of reverence.

Again, the introduction to the office, the chapters, the prayers, the blessings, the versicles after the responsories, and the responsories of the hours must be said standing, and with the capuce down.

Again, the psalm *Laudate Dominum de coelis*[20], and the gospel canticles, namely, the *Magnificat, Nunc dimittis* and *Benedictus,* must always be said standing.

Again, the *Pater Noster* and the rest of the *preces* must never be said sitting.

---

20 This is psalm 148, but Humbert is including psalms 149-50, since all three are said at the end of Lauds with only one *Gloria Patri.*

Again, once an hour has been begun, nothing extraneous to it should be done or said until it is finished, unless there be some great necessity; and if some notable interruption occurs, it should be begun again.

Again, when the office is said, there is no place for casualness or humour; it should all be said in a mature manner, and seriously.

Again, just as if a brother should not come to choir if he were not wearing shoes or were in some other way not properly attired, nor should he say the office privately in such a state, unless some reasonable necessity excuses and requires it.

These, then, and like things are to be observed in order that the office may be recited reverently.

Commentary on the CONSTITUTIONS, c.35.

IV

Of Bows & Genuflections

1. Of the various ways of humbling the body before God

IN ORDER BETTER TO UNDERSTAND WHAT IS said in this chapter, know that three things must come together in order that we may accomplish the divine cult worthily. These are the heart, the mouth, and the body.

The worship of the heart consists in faith, hope, charity, and suchlike spiritual things. These lift up the mind to God. But these are not discussed by human rules, which treat instead of outward actions.

The worship of the lips consists in the liturgy of the Church, which has already been discussed.

The worship of the body consists in humbling it before God, and humbling it in God's sight before images and similar things. It is this worship of which we must now speak.

There are three ways of humbling our bodies. We may bow deeply, as far as the waist. This is called bowing. Secondly, we may be humbled to our knees, which is called kneeling or genuflexion. Finally, we may be humbled as far as our ankles. This is called prostration.

These are the three immersions which Ezechiel knew when he went into the downward-flowing river of humility, now to his ankles, now to his knees, now to his waist (Ez. 47:1–5).[21]

But note that there are two kinds of bow. The first is the profound bow as far as the knees. The other is moderate, being somewhat less that the first.

There are also two ways of kneeling. The first is with one's body held straight and resting on the knees. This may be called

21 Fr Hering ends this chapter here.

a straight genuflexion. The other is with one's body sloping forwards, which may be called an inclined genuflexion.

Again, there are two kinds of prostration. One is made with one's whole body, and is sometimes called a *venia*. The other is made with one's body while kneeling, and this is the same as the inclined genuflexion. So when the body is humbled in this last manner, the Constitutions call it sometimes genuflexion, sometimes prostration.

Commentary on the CONSTITUTIONS, c.51.

---

2. *What reasons are there for bowing?*

THERE ARE MANY REASONS WHY MEN MAY bow. Sometimes it is done from reverence. Reverence arises from the consideration of another's greatness, which makes one shrink back into one's own littleness, and this is made manifest by a bow. It was for this reason that Jacob's handmaids and their children bowed down before Esau: *Then the handmaids and their children came near and bowed themselves* (Gen. 33:6), that is, bowing before Esau to show him reverence.

Sometimes the bow is made from thanksgiving. For every gift weighs down the one who receives it. But whatever weighs something down causes it to bend, as the fruit does the branch. So the one who is grateful for a gift that he has received bends himself down, as if to show that the gift is not small, but great enough to cause him to bend. It was for this reason that Abraham's servant bowed down, as he thanked God for the success of his journey. *The man bowed himself down, saying: Blessed be God* (Gen. 24:26).

Sometimes the bow is made to lend strength to prayer. For it is humility that makes a prayer powerful, and so it is good for one who is praying to humble himself by bowing. It was for this reason that those people bowed of whom it is written: *They bowed down, and adored God* (2 Esd. 8:6).

But sometimes one bows in order to magnify another. For one way in which we magnify another is to stand in his sight with our faces downwards, like the humble Virgin who said: *My soul doth magnify the Lord* (Lk. 1:46). It was in this way that Isaac willed Jacob's brothers to bow down before him, to show that Jacob was their lord, and that his house was greater than theirs. For Isaac said: *Be thou lord of thy brethren, and let thy mother's children bow down before thee* (Gen. 27:29).

Sometimes a bow is a sign of obedience. *Bowing his head,* that is, as a sign that He was obedient unto death, *he gave up the ghost* (Jn. 19:30).

Sometimes one bows in order to benefit from a blessing, which is a grace given to the humble. So the deacon chants the words *Humiliate vos ad benedictionem*. It is in this way that the heavens, that is, heavenly men, are bowed down by God, and the Lord comes down to them as a result of His blessing. *He bowed the heavens and came down* (Ps. 17:10).

Sometimes a bow is made from shame, as with the publican, who for his great shame did not dare to lift his eyes to heaven (Lk. 18:9–14).

Sometimes one bows to show that one is humbling oneself. *He that shall bow down his eyes, he shall be saved* (Job 22:29); that is, the one who bows down with humbled eyes will be saved.

These various reasons explain why we make the bows prescribed by custom or by the Constitutions. Thus the first motive, reverence, explains the bows made whenever we pass before the altar or the Cross or an image of our Lady or of one of the saints; and also the bows that we make when an eminent person or one worthy of veneration passes before us, or we pass before them; and the bow made to the altar in offering candles on the day of the Purification.

It is from thanksgiving that a bow is made when the name of Blessed Dominic is mentioned in a prayer, and why, after the first verse of a psalm has been completed, both the one who begins the antiphon and the one who intones the psalm bow towards the altar, and why the lector does the same after a reading.

The third motive, that of lending strength to prayer, applies to the bows made at the *Pater Noster* and the *Credo*, when they are said at the start of Office, and during the *preces* and the prayer for the Church and the *suscipe deprecationem nostram* in the Gloria, and in certain other prayers.

We bow, fourthly, to magnify the Trinity at the *Gloria Patri* and during the last stanza of the hymns and during the penultimate verse of the *Benedicite*.

From obedience we bow, fifthly, whenever something is enjoined upon us, whether individually or as a community.

Again, there are several times when a bow is made in order to benefit from a blessing. Thus a bow is made when one requests a blessing before a reading, and in Lent at the last post-communion, when a blessing is given to the people, and when the blessing is given in the sermon. And this is the sixth reason.

Again, seventhly, when someone is late coming into choir, then he must bow in between the stalls in the midst of the brethren, as it were paying the tribute of his shame. The same is done for a mistake committed when reading or singing.

Finally, one bows when naming the Blessed Virgin, when saying *et homo factus est* in the Creed, and when receiving ashes. These bows are made for the eighth motive, that is, to humble ourselves.

And let no one disparage these bows, as if they had only recently been brought into the divine cult by religious. For they were observed of old; so it is written: *And all the asssembly blessed the Lord the God of their fathers: and they bowed themselves and worshipped Him* (1 Par. 19). And that was in the days of King David.

Commentary on the CONSTITUTIONS, c.52

---

3. Of kneeling

THERE ARE LIKEWISE MANY REASONS FOR kneeling. Sometimes it is done from reverence. So all the servants of King Assuerus apart from Mardechai knelt before Aman when they came to the palace (Est. 3:2). It is for this reason that we kneel at the words *Salve, sancta Parens*, and at the verse *O crux, Ave*, and sometimes before greater prelates when we wish to make some appeal more urgently.

Thus Stephen also knelt as he prayed for his enemies (Acts 7:59), and we kneel for the same reason at the beginning of Office, and at the *preces*, and whenever *Flectamus genua* is said.

We also kneel in Lent at the words *Adiuva nos, Deus, salutaris noster*, and at the words *Sancte Deus, sancte fortis, sancte et misericors Salvator* in the antiphon at Compline.

Sometimes a man kneels from devotion, since it is a way of manifesting the love he has within himself. Thus holy men kneel one to the other when they meet or part. It was for this reason that Solomon knelt before God and before the multitude of the people, showing the love that he had in his heart because of all the favours he had received. *Kneeling down in the presence of all the multitude of Israel . . . he said: O Lord God of Israel, there is no God like thee in heaven or in earth: who keepest covenant and mercy with thy servants* (2 Par. 6:13–14). So we sometimes kneel from devotion before good men, and privately before an altar, or a cross, or an image.

Sometimes kneeling is done to manifest humility. This was why the third captain of fifty knelt before Elias, after the first two captains had spoken to him proudly (4 Kings 1:13). It is for this reason that we kneel at the *Veni, Sancte Spiritus,* humbling ourselves so that the One who rests upon the humble may come to us.

There are other times when we kneel not from one only of these motives, but from two or more. This is true of our kneeling in adoration of the Cross on Palm Sunday and Good Friday, and of our kneeling before the Body of our Lord, and sometime before relics of the saints.

Thus kneeling must not be rejected when the divine cult is in question. It is done on the authority of kings, Levites, priests, prophets, and of our Lord Himself, and His apostles.

Concerning kings: *Kneeling down in the presence of all the multitude... he said: O Lord God of Israel, there is no God like thee* (2 Par. 6:13–14). This was in the temple.

Concerning Levites: *They,* that is the Levites, *praised the Lord with great joy, and bowing the knee adored* (2 Par. 29:30).

Concerning priests: Esdras the priest says: *I fell upon my knees, and spread out my hands to the Lord my God, and said: My God, I am confounded and ashamed to lift up my face to thee* (1 Esd. 9:5–6).

Concerning prophets, it is said through Isaias: *For every knee shall be bowed to me* (Is. 45:24). What is said here was fulfilled in deed by Daniel: *Opening his windows in his upper chamber towards Jerusalem, he knelt down three times a day and adored, and gave thanks before his God* (Dan. 6:10).

Concerning our Lord, it is written: *Kneeling down, he prayed the longer* (Lk. 22:41).

Concerning the apostles: *For this cause I bow my knee to the Father of our Lord Jesus Christ . . . that he would grant you to be strengthened with might* (Eph. 3:14). And it is recorded of Blessed Bartholomew that he prayed to God kneeling down one hundred times during the day and one hundred times during the night. Of James the Less it is related that his knees became as hard as those of a camel, so much did he kneel.

Note that whilst we sometimes kneel on one knee before great men, yet before God we must kneel with both, because of the greater reverence which is due to Him. *Solomon rose from before the altar of the Lord: for he had fixed both knees on the ground* (3 Kings 8:54).

---

4. Of Prostrations

PROSTRATIONS, ALSO, ARE PERFORMED FOR various reasons. Sometimes they are made in order to receive a punishment. *If the offender be worthy of stripes: they shall lay him down, and shall cause him to be beaten before them* (Deut. 25:2). So we also prostrate to receive the discipline.

Sometimes it is done to show readiness to obey a command. *Before him the Ethiopians shall fall down* (Ps. 71:9), to show, that is, that they are ready to obey those commands of his which they had formerly resisted. So we do when we receive a charge that is laid upon us.

Sometimes a prostration is made in order to obtain mercy. *Semei, falling down before the king, said to him: impute not to me, my lord, the iniquity, nor remember the injuries of thy servant.* (2 Kings 19:19). Thus we do when we seek pardon from a brother whom we have offended, and when we go to confession, and on entering into the Order when we prostrate ourselves and seek mercy from God and the Order.

Sometimes it is done in thanksgiving. *Then they lying prostrate for three hours upon their face, blessed God* (Tob. 12:22). Thus we do when we have finished the reading, prostrating ourselves and so to speak blessing God for the graces given to us from reading.[22]

Sometimes a prostration is made in order to receive a blessing. That is what the early fathers did, prostrating themselves before one another and saying, "Bless me, father", as we read in the *Lives of the Fathers.* This is what we do when we prostrate ourselves to receive the blessing before going on a journey and when we return.

Sometimes it is done in penitence or from sorrow. *Judith putting on haircloth, laid ashes on her head: and falling down prostrate before the Lord, she cried to the Lord* (Jud. 9:1). This is what we do when we recite the penitential psalms on the Tuesday[23] at the beginning of Lent, and on Maundy Thursday, and secretly, whenever we are moved by compunction, according to the text: *Come, let us adore and fall down: and weep before the Lord that made us* (Ps. 94:6).

Sometimes it is done in adoration. *And falling down they adored him* (Matt. 2:11). This is what we do at the office.

Sometimes it is from reverence. So Abraham fell to the ground before the three men who appeared to him (Gen. 18:2; cf. 17:3). This is what we do when we make a prostration before a relic or some other sacred thing.

Sometime it is done from humility, like Peter, who on seeing the haul of fish fell down before Jesus's knees and said: *Depart from me, for I am a sinful man* (Lk. 5:8).

But sometimes one and the same prostration may be done from a variety of causes, such as a prostration before the body of our Lord, or in the adoration of the Cross.

22 That is, the readings at matins.
23 *Sic: 'feria tertia'.*

The worshippers of Christ must not fail to perform such prostrations in the divine cult. For we read that the Jews used to make
them with great diligence: *All the children of Israel . . . falling
down with their faces to the ground, upon the stone pavement,
adored and praised the Lord* (2 Par. 7:3).

Again, idolaters do the same. *All the nations, tribes, and lan-
guages fell down and adored the golden statue* (Dan. 3:7).

Again, we read of the demons, *And the unclean spirits, when
they saw him, fell down before him and they cried, saying: Thou
art the Son of God* (Mk. 3:11).

So if the Jews in their cult and the idolaters in their rites made
prostrations with such devotion, and if even the demons made
them before Christ, how much more should they be performed
with supreme devotion in the Christian cult?

Again, the twenty-four elders represent the entirety of the
saints. But it is recorded of them that *the four and twenty
ancients fell down before him that sitteth on the throne, and
adored him that liveth for ever and ever* (Apoc. 4:10).

Again, it is written of the angels: *All the angels stood round
about the throne, and the ancients, and the four living creatures;
and they fell down before the throne upon their faces, and adored
God* (Apoc. 7:11).

Again, it is written of Christ Himself: *He fell upon his face,
praying* (Matt. 26:39).

So if all the saints, and in fact the very angels, and indeed
Christ Himself make such devout prostrations, how can they be
neglected by men who are wise of spirit?

From all that has been said it is clear that bows, genuflexions
and prostrations must not in any way be omitted from the divine
cult by men who are devoted to God.

Yet notice that all these ways of humbling the body without
must correspond to something within. For we must not only
bow down outwardly, but also bow down our hearts within:
Incline your hearts to the Lord the God of Israel (Jos. 24:23).

Likewise, we must bend the knees of our heart, according to
the example of Mannases, who said: *And now I bend the knees*

of my heart, beseeching goodness from thee, O Lord (Prayer of Mannases 1:11).

Again, we must prostrate ourselves in heart, according to the text: *My soul hath cleaved to the pavement* (Ps. 118:25), as if to say, I cleave to the pavement not only by prostrating my body, but also with my soul.

Again, we make many bows, genuflexions and prostrations from one and the same cause, as well as making one and the same such action from several different causes, as has been said already.

Again, there are some that we make because we must, such as those which are written down or commonly performed; and there are others that we make from devotion, namely the bows, genuflexions and prostrations that we make in private, or independently of the community.

But among private actions there are some which are made by certain seculars, but which religion does not approve, such as prostrating oneself with one's arms extended in the form of a cross, kissing the ground. For these are unbecoming, and also sometimes harm the body imprudently because of the coldness of the ground.

Again, some of these ways of humbling the body are acts of *latria*, the reverence that is due to God alone, and these are the ones that we make only to Him; others belong to the reverence that is a form of honour shown to a creature from some reasonable cause, and these are the ones that we make to prelates and to other creatures.[24]

Commentary on the Constitutions, *c.54.*

---

5. Of various bodily actions pertaining to the adoration of God

A S WELL AS THE THREE WAYS OF HUMBLING the body of which we have already spoken, there are yet other bodily observances included in the divine cult. Thus, adoration is

24 The last two paragraphs are not included in Fr Hering's selection from Humbert.

sometimes shown by casting down one's face, as a sign of shame, and so it is said: *They shall worship thee with their face toward the earth* (Is. 49:23). Sometimes it is shown by raising up one's eyes, following the example of our Lord, of whom it is said: *Lifting up his eyes to heaven, he said: Father, the hour is come, glorify thy Son* (Jn. 17:1). This is done as a sign of the heart's intention.

Again, sometimes we stand to adore. This is done from reverence, in accordance with what is written of the saints and the angels: *After this I saw a great multitude which no man could number . . . standing before the throne and in sight of the Lamb*, and a little after: *And all the angels stood round about the throne* (Apoc. 7:9, 11). Sometimes we sit. This is a concession to the weakness of our nature. But it is not wholly to be blamed, since the Apostles were seated when they received the Holy Ghost, and it is clear from the Church's chant that they were praying when they received Him. Therefore, they were sitting when they prayed and received the Holy Ghost. Thus the Holy Ghost does not always hold in horror the one who sits to pray.

Again, we sometimes turn our faces toward the altar. This is a sign of our intention, which goes out toward God. Thus the Bridegroom says to the Church: *Shew me thy face*, and then, *Let thy voice sound in my ears* (Cant. 2:14). Sometimes we turn our faces to each other, as a sign of the unanimity which we have in praising God, like to the cherubim who for the same reason *their faces being turned, look one towards the other on the propitiatory* (Ex. 25:20).

Again, we sometimes let our hands fall, according to the text: *When a voice came from above the firmament, that was over the heads of the four living creatures, they stood, and let down their wings* (Ez. 1:25), reckoning their own power as naught. This is done to show one's lowliness. So the gloss says on this verse, "They stood in contemplation, and let down their wings".

Sometimes the hands are raised, according to the teaching of the Apostle, where he says: *I will that men pray in every place, lifting up pure hands* (1 Tim. 2:8). This practice should not be spurned or neglected, since *when Moses lifted up his hands*,

Israel overcame: but if he let them down a little, Amalec overcame (Ex. 17:11).

Sometimes the hands are spread apart. *I stretched forth my hands to thee* (Ps. 142:6). This is done in particular at the altar, where the priest acts in the person of Christ.

Sometimes the hands are joined. In one version it says: *With their hands joined they shall worship thee, and shall make supplication to thee* (Is. 45:14). This was said of Cyrus, who was acting in the person of Christ.

Again, sometimes the hood of the capuce is put down, in particular when someone is reciting something in choir, whether he is reading or singing or reciting the prayer. For if the four and twenty ancients cast down their crowns when they prayed (Apoc. 4), how much more should we put down our capuces. So the Apostle says: *Every man praying or prophesying with his head covered, disgraceth his head* (1 Cor. 11:4).

Again, sometimes the breast is struck, following the example of the publican of whom it is said: *He struck his breast, saying: O God, be merciful to me a sinner* (Lk. 18:13).

Sometimes the sign of the Cross is made. So on the text: *Mark Tau on the foreheads of the men that sigh* (Ez. 9:4), the gloss says, "The letter Tau is in the form of a cross, which is often traced on the foreheads of Christian men, in the strength of which they are marked".

One should know that the best posture for prayer is to kneel with one's head and eyes raised up, and one's hands joined. Experienced men know this. For the soul quickly clothes herself with the body's dispositions, on account of the close union between the two. Kneeling implies humility, while raising the head and eyes leads to the raising up of the heart, since the soul easily follows the dispositions of the body, because of the connection which she has with it. The joining of the hands expresses love. And there is nothing more profitable in prayer than humility, intention and love.

Profound bows should be made before the altar, on account of the holiness of the altar, which receives a fuller consecration than anything else in the church.

Again, they should be performed on account of the relics and the holy images, which are normally on the altar or near it; and most of all because of our Lord's Body, which is reserved there also. Of this last point it is said in Is. 17:7 *In that day,* that is, in the time of grace, *man shall bow down himself to his Maker, and he shall not look to the altars which his hands have made.* We therefore bow before Him, paying our homage to His great majesty, and giving thanks for the great blessing of the Incarnation, and judging it worthy that we be humbled as we reflect on that humility. This profound bow should be done both from reverence to our Lord's body and also out of reverence for the convent; for these are the two reasons for profound bows. Therefore, when we pass in front of other altars or images, or in front of the high altar when the community is not there, although we should always bow, yet according to a custom which takes its origin from this constitution,[25] we do not have to bow so deeply, since these two reasons are not then both present.

Commentary on the CONSTITUTIONS, c. 55

---

6. Of the Sign of the Cross

To UNDERSTAND WHY WE FORTIFY OURSELVES with the sign of the cross at the start of the office, consider that although the demons seek to obstruct all good works, they particularly try to hinder prayer. Hence, abba Agatho says in the *Lives of the Fathers*: "Whenever a man wishes to pray, the hostile demons make haste to prevent him, for they know that they are brought to confusion by nothing so much as by prayer." This is why, whenever the brethren come together to pray, the demons also come together to obstruct them. Thus, when a certain demon told Macarius that he was going to the office of vigils, where the brethren were gathered, and Macarius asked the demon what

25 Humbert is commenting on the passage in the constitutions which says: "When the matins of the little office of our Lady have been said, and the brethren come into choir, they should bow deeply to the altar."

business he had at that vigil, the demon answered that no gathering of monks performed its office without there being demons present. This is told in the *Lives of the Fathers*. Hence, it is written in Jb. 2:1: *On a certain day, when the sons of God had come and were standing before the Lord, Satan also was present among them.*

When the devil intrudes himself among those who are praying, he sometimes attempts to entice them by suggesting pretexts for abandoning their prayer. Hence, Gregory relates in his *Dialogues* that blessed Benedict beheld a certain monk who could not persevere at prayer being dragged of by a black boy, and that having himself prayed for two days, blessed Benedict caused two others to see this sight also.

Now, sometimes, when the devil cannot entice people to abandon prayer, he seeks to impede it. In the *Lives of the Fathers* it is recorded that Blessed Macarius saw foreign boys[26] flitting about around the brethren as they prayed; some monks they poked in the eyes, and these monks fell asleep; they put their fingers into the mouths of others, and these ones started yawning; before some, they turned themselves into the appearance of women, or into some other appearance. They sat on the backs of some and, Macarius supposed, made it burdensome for them to remain in choir. They sat on the heads of others, and seemed to him to tempt these ones to pride. And indeed later on, when these monks had opened their consciences to him, Macarius found it all as he had guessed.

From this we can conclude that the devil seeks to obstruct those who pray, either by leading them away from prayer if he can, or, if he cannot, by inducing sleep, or else prompting them to certain actions or sending them certain thoughts, or making them weary, or drawing them into some presumption of spirit.

It is clear that the sign of the cross is mighty against these enemies. As Origen says, "the power of constant meditation on Christ's cross is so great that if it be faithfully kept in our heart, the whole host of death is put to flight as we recall it". But death is the devil itself, as it is said in Apoc. 6:6.

26   *Pueros aethiopes.*

Again, 1 Pet. 4:1: *Christ therefore having suffered in the flesh, be you also armed with the same thought*; that is, of the passion and the cross.

Again, it is said in Ez. 9:6 that the exterminating angels did not touch those who had the 'Tau' marked upon their forehead.

Again, Gregory relates in the *Dialogues* that when a certain Jew was going to sleep in a pagan temple and made the sign of the cross despite having no faith, the devil, who had been approaching him, fled and cried out: "An empty vessel, but one that is marked!"

Therefore, if the memory of the cross, the thought of the passion, the shape of the cross, nay, the very tracing of the sign performed without faith, is such a powerful defence against these enemies, how much more will the cross be when it is made with faith and with the thought of the passion. Hence, in Apoc. 7:2–3 it is said that the angel with the seal of the living God cried out to the four angels to whom it was given to harm the earth, that they should do no harm, until the servants of God were signed on their foreheads; and the gloss explains this as referring to the sign of the cross. Therefore, we are fortified by the sign of the cross at the start of the office, and by its power we are defended during the office from the enemies who attack so fiercely at that time. Thus, we make this sign when we say: *Deus, in adiutorium* etc.

But note that we do not make this sign only at the start of the office, but in many other places. Sometimes this is done from personal devotion, as some do when they go to bed, or begin to preach or read or pray or eat or finish eating, and so forth.

Sometimes it is done from the common custom of secular churches, for example at the end of the gospel and the creed and the *Gloria in excelsis*, and at the *Benedictus qui venit*, when this is chanted at Mass. Master John Beleth says that we are also accustomed to sign ourselves at the evangelical canticles, when they are sung; but since this is not a universal custom in all places, some observe it, and others do not.

Sometimes the sign of the cross is made in accordance with something in our Constitutions, as is laid down in various places in the *Ordinarium* and in the Constitutions.

Now, the cross is made sometimes simply as a sign. For example, we sign ourselves at the start of the gospel upon the breast, the mouth and the forehead, as a sign that we have the wisdom of the cross in our mind, that we profess it by our mouth, and that we will not be ashamed to confess it publicly. Rabanus says: "The cross is the wisdom of the foolish"; that is, of those whom the world reckons foolish.

Sometimes, however, the sign of the cross is made for the sake of some effect. This may be to confer something good, as when a blessing is given with the sign of the cross. For the Cross is that by which the grace of justification has been granted unto the world. Anselm says in his oration about the Cross: "By thee, human nature has been justified". Or it may be to obtain some sanctification, as when food or branches or candles and so on are blessed. For the Cross is what sanctifies. Hence, bishop John (Chrysostom) says in his sermon for Good Friday: "Today, the Cross has been set up, and the world has been sanctified." Or it may be to obtain some deliverance; and so, the same bishop says: "The Cross has been erected, and the demons scattered." Hence, the apostle says in 1 Cor. 1:30: *He is made unto us wisdom and justice and sanctification and redemption*; and this happened through the Cross. For His servants do not reckon that they know anything except Him crucified, which relates to the first point, namely, to wisdom. Again, they do not have the grace of justice from anywhere save by the wood through which comes justice, and this relates to the second point. Again, if water gained a power to sanctify from having touched our Lord's body, how did not the cross do so all the more? And so it is called holy and sanctifying, which relates to the third point, sanctification. Again, it is the rod of His power by which He rules in the midst of His foes, and redeems us from them, and this relates to the fourth point, that is, redemption.

Commentary on the CONSTITUTIONS, c.57.

PART III

Devotion Towards the
BLESSED VIRGIN MARY

I

Why the *Salve* is
Sung after Compline

AT THE START OF THE ORDER, WHEN THE
Constitutions were first drawn up, the *Salve* procession did not
yet exist. But when a certain brother at Bologna was being tor-
mented by the devil, the brethren decided that the *Salve Regina*
should be sung after compline, to obtain his liberation, and so it
happened. A commemoration of the angels, using the responsory
Te sanctum Dominum was introduced at Paris for the same reason,
but later on a chapter decided to give up this commemoration in
order to prevent the office from becoming too long. The procession of the Blessed Virgin, however, to which the brethren had
a greater devotion, was never omitted once it had been begun.
Master Jordan has recounted that a certain religious, who was
worthy of belief, told him that he had often seen the Blessed
Virgin prostrating herself before her Son and praying to Him for
the preservation of the Order, when the brethren were singing
the words, *Eia, ergo, advocata nostra*. And although nothing
of all this has been written down in the Constitutions or the
Ordinarium, the memory of it has been preserved over a long
period of time by the use of the *Salve Regina*; for even outside
choir, the brethren always use this antiphon.

In the course of time, it was decided that other antiphons
might be used, to prevent people from growing bored of this

one, and this was written in the *Ordinarium*. This was when mention was made in writing for the first time of this procession, which had until then been simply a matter of custom. And since it was then written in the *Ordinarium*, there was no need to put anything about it into the Constitutions. This is why no mention of is made of this procession there, even though it should be carried out with great devotion by the brethren of the Order of Preachers in perpetuity, and without interruption.

To understand the reason for this procession, we must realise that since we have many great affairs to conduct in the heavenly court, each of us must strive to have some saint, or some special helpers, who will be his patrons for the affairs that he wishes to promote in that court, as happens also in the courts of this world. Hence in Job 5:1 it is said to Job in his need: *Turn to some one of the saints,* that is, who will be your helper with God. But among all those in that court, the Blessed Virgin is the most excellent of patrons, and hence she is called the Star of the Sea, which more than all the other stars helps those who are making their crossing. Lk. 1:27: *The virgin's name was Mary,* that is, the star of the sea.

There are many things that make her patronage so excellent. First of all, the patronage of those who are most powerful at a court is better; and she is such. Bernard says: "She cannot lack the power of interceding, since she is the Queen of heaven." Hence, in Ecclus. 24:15 it is said in her person: *My power in Jerusalem,* that is, in supernal glory.

Again, a person's patronage is better insofar as he is more familiarly known to the lord from which he wishes to obtain something. But what closer familiarity can there be than between the Son and the Mother? Bernard: "How familiar with God art thou made, O Lady! How close; nay, how intimate!" Hence, it is said in Ps. 44:10 *The queen stood on thy right hand,* that is, being more familiar with thee than all the others in the court.

Again, the more skilful someone is at obtaining his requests and arranging business, the better is his patronage. But she is like this. Bernard says: "The Mother shows to the Son her breast", that is, to obtain her request. What energy she uses! Hence, she is prefigured in 1 Kings 25 by Abigail, whose name means "my father exults". For no other daughter of Adam ever gave to him such reason for exultation as she has done. Abigail, as is said there, was very prudent, and by her prudence she placated King David, and freed her foolish husband from death. And ah, how many fools has the Blessed Virgin freed from death, and daily frees, by placating the King of heaven!

Again, the more someone is feared by one's enemy, the better is his patronage. But she to the enemy is *terrible as an army set in array*, as it says in Cant. 6:3, 9.

Of great value, therefore, is the patronage of her who is powerful in the heavenly court, familiar to the king of that court, skilled in arranging affairs, and terrible to the enemy.

We may have great hope that her patronage will be easily gained. For she is not lacking compassion or hard toward those who come to her; no, she is found to be entirely gentle. Bernard: "Why should human weakness fear to come to Mary? There is nothing harsh about her, nothing dreadful; she is sweetness itself, full of loving-kindness and grace, full of gentleness and mercy." Hence, in Cant. 6:3, it is said: *Thou art sweet.*

Again, more is to be hoped from the help of one who is more indebted to the needy person. But she is much indebted to sinners, since it is on account of them that she possesses all that excellence of hers. Augustine says in his prayer to her: "A strange bond binds us to thee and thee to us; thou hast what thou art for our sake, and we have what we are through thee." Hence, in Is. 11:1 she is called a rod come forth from the stock of Jesse, a name that means 'fire'; for from the fire of that great love which God had for the world, He came to her, and so the world was the cause of her being.

Again, just as the judge appoints a counsel for unfortunate persons, so she has been assigned as patron and counsel to us unfortunates. Likewise, it was divinely arranged that Esther should be raised to the royal throne, so that she might be the advocate for the Jewish people. Hence, it is said in Est. 4:14:

Who knoweth whether thou art not therefore come to the kingdom, that thou mightest be ready in such a time as this?—that is, to intercede for her people. And what is written there in the form of a question is in fact the truth. For just as in the papal court, poor folk come with confidence to the man whom the pope has appointed to be the promoter of the causes of the poor, so we should come confidently to the Blessed Virgin, since it belongs to her by reason of her office to arrange our affairs.

Again, more is hoped from the aid of one whose loving aid has already been demonstrated by much experience. And she is such a one, as is attested by innumerable proofs. For who has come to her, and not been helped? Bernard says: "If there be anyone, O blessed Virgin, who has called upon thy mercy in his needs and can recall that it failed him, then let that man not speak of it!" And notice that she helps everyone. Bernard: "Affectionate in her compassion, and effective in her aid, she aids everyone." Hence, in Ecclus. 24:19 it is said: *As an olive tree in the plains,* not "in the gardens"; and so all may share in the fruit.

Again, she helps in all cases. Bernard: "She has been made all things to all men, so that everyone may receive from her fullness. The prisoner receives ransom; the sick, healing; the sorrowful, comfort; the sinner, pardon; the just man, grace. She takes pity on the needs of all, in the greatness of her love." And so it was said to her in Lk. 1:28: *Ave*; that is, "without woe", for she frees from every form of wretchedness.

Again, she helps everywhere, that is, on earth, in heaven, and in hell. Bernard says: "The breadth of her mercy fills the earth; the heights of the heavenly city of Jerusalem have found the one who restores them; the deep places where they sat in darkness and in the shadow of death have found their Redeemer." This, according to Bernard, is the meaning of the phrase "in the midst of the earth", in the passage in Ps. 73:12 which says: *He hath wrought salvation in the midst of the earth.* For to her, as to the middle, do they look who dwell in heaven, and in the underworld; those who went before us, and we who now are, and those who will come after us.

Again, she always helps. Bernard says: "The length of her mercy helps all those who call upon her, down to the last day." Hence, in Ecclus. 24:14, it is said: *Until the world to come I shall not cease*, that is, cease to help all men.

Therefore, it is plain how much can be hoped for from her aid, if she is faithfully invoked, since she is gentle and patient with those who come to her, since she is so bound to help us, for this belongs to her in virtue of her office, and it has been proved by such long experience! For this reason, Paul says in Heb. 4:16: *Let us go with confidence to the throne of grace.* For she is the throne of God's grace, for from her the manifold graces of God go forth to mankind. We call that 'the throne of grace' from which grace goes forth.

Therefore, since her patronage is so powerful and may so easily be had, her patronage is to be preferred beyond that of all others. That is why we daily make a procession in her honour, so that we may always have her as our patroness in heaven.

Now, from events that occurred at the beginning of our Order, we have many reasons to suppose that she is the special patroness of our Order, along with Blessed Dominic, its father and master. I heard with my own ears from a Cistercian monk, who was certainly a most reliable man, that before the beginning of our Order, when Pope Innocent had sent the twelve abbots to the region of the Albigenses, one of the abbots as he journeyed entered a certain village and heard about a man there who had died and had been brought back to life. A large number of people went to see the man, and the abbot also sent the monk who was travelling with him to enquire about the matter. The monk, finding things as he had been told, asked the man who had come back to life what he had seen in the other world. The man said among other things that he had seen the Blessed Virgin kneeling before her Son for three days and three nights, making intercession for the world. When her Son, our Lord Jesus Christ, resisted her, on account of the world's ingratitude, and the evil which it rendered Him for good, she in turn insisted in her prayer that He might deal with it not in accord with its deserts but with His mercy. Finally, she gained this answer: on account of her prayers He would delay to do justice to the world, and would send it still some people who would warn it to correct itself, and that if it corrected itself, He would spare it. A little time afterward, this Order came into being, and so that good monk supposed that it had been brought into the world at the prayers of the Blessed Virgin.

Again, is it not she who restored brother Reginald of blessed memory back to health, anointing his feet in preparation for the gospel of peace? By his example and preaching our Order grew greatly.

Again, during my novitiate, if I remember correctly, I heard that at the start of the Order, a certain holy anchoress had seen some of our young brethren travelling about in the world; and being in her oratory, before a picture of the Blessed Virgin, she thought about this, wondering if it were possible for them to avoid the sins of the world, especially since they were young men and had such a handsome habit. And she heard a voice, as if from the painting, saying to her: "Be not afraid for these brothers, for I have taken them into my charge." And she showed her a host of friars preachers beneath her mantle.

Hence, from these things, and from many others which are recorded in the *Lives of the Brethren,* it appears that she is the special mother of this Order, which exists to praise, bless and preach her Son, and that she produced it, promotes it, and defends it. For this reason, Blessed Dominic commended the Order to her, as to its special patroness, as is recorded in the *New Legend.*[27] And this is why we recommend ourselves daily to her, as our mother, by our procession, as we do to Blessed Dominic, our father, by a commemoration, having them both as our special patrons in heaven.

Commentary on the CONSTITUTIONS, c.42.

27 This refers to the new biography of St. Dominic (known as a *legenda* in Latin) written by Constantine of Orvieto, OP, in the mid-1240s.

11

Why Saturday is Assigned to the Blessed Virgin

IT IS GOOD TO KNOW WHY THOSE WHO ARE
devoted to the Blessed Virgin honour her more on Saturdays
than on other days. Consider, then, that our Lord is said to have
rested on the Sabbath; again, He rested in her as in His tabernacle. Therefore, the sabbath and the Virgin are in harmony, for
Saturday is the time of our Lord's rest, and she is the place of it.

Again, the work of creation, that is, of nature, was finished on
the Saturday; in her, the work of re-creation, that is, of grace, was
finished. Bernard says: "In thee, and through thee, O most kind
Lady, the hand of the Maker recreated all that He had created".
Thus, she and Saturday agree in regard to completion.

Again, the day of Sabbath was blessed more than the other
days, and so Gen. 2:3 says: *God blessed the seventh day*. Likewise,
she is blessed above all women.

Again, the Saturday was holier than the other days, and so in
the same place it is said: *He sanctified it*. And she is holier than all.

So it is fitting that she who is blessed above all and holier than
all should be more specially honoured on the holier day.

Again, just as Saturday is a midpoint between Friday, which is
the penal day, and Sunday, which is the day of joy, and no one
can pass from that penal day to the day of joy except through
Saturday, so can no one pass from the penalties of this world to
the joys of heaven, unless through her, the Mediatrix of the world.

Again, as the Fathers say, when the others failed on the Sabbath, her faith remained.

Again, she is found often to have worked miracles on the Sabbath. John Beleth gives the example of a picture of Mary, where
the veil was lifted on the Saturday. And many similar things
have occurred.

[87]

Therefore, these are the seven reasons why we serve her more especially on Saturdays, carrying out her office in full in the church, solemnly and devoutly. And in the Church's services, a sequence is sung proper to that day, which mentions all these reasons why Saturday is particularly attributed to her:

Iubilemus in hac die
Quam Reginae coeli piae
Dicavit Ecclesia.

Haec est dies in qua sua
Vota tibi, Virgo, tua
Reddit haec familia.

Omne saeculum, omni die
Servi Virgini Mariae:
Sed in hac devotius.

In hac psallas, in hac ores,
In hac laudes et labores,
Et cantes iucundius.

Virgo quae non habet parem
Diem sibi singularem
Non iniuste vindicat.

O quam digne sibi dari
Diem hunc et consecrari
Res inspecta praedicat!

Hodiernae lux diei
Dies fuit requiei
Plasmatoris omnium.

Sic quievit in Maria,
Dum ipsius in hac via
Virgo fit hospitium.

Cunctae tunc sunt creaturae
Factae dum opus naturae
Complet Deus hodie.

Universa tunc refecit,
Dum in Matre qui nos fecit
Complet opus gratiae.

Dies olim benedicta,
Dies quoque sancta dicta
Fuit ista septima.

Quam benedicta dicaris
Scimus, Virgo singularis,
Et quam sis sanctissima.

Dum transis ad gaudiosum
Diem, relinquens poenosum,
Dies est haec media.

Haec de poenis nos educit
Mediatrix, et adducit
Ad superna gaudia.

In hac die dum desperat
Grex pusillus qui tunc erat
Fidem tenet firmius.

In hac die suspirantes
Ad se, seque deprecantes
Obaudit frequentius.

Veneremus ergo, fratres,
Ut sanxerunt sancti patres,
In hac die Virginem.

Exorantes ut conducat
Nos hic, et tandem perducat
Ad illam dulcedinem. Amen.

Commentary on the CONSTITUTIONS, c.24

The prayer of Blessed Dominic, according to the witnesses at the process of canonisation.

"He (Dominic) wished always, when travelling, to discuss God, or to teach or read or pray. And even when he was travelling, he offered Mass more or less daily, if he could find a church. And when he sang Mass, he shed many tears, as the witness himself saw. And when he came to any hostel, if there was a church there, he always went to pray in the church. And nearly always, when he was away from a priory, when he heard the monasteries begin to ring their bells for matins, he would get up and rouse the brethren, and celebrate the whole divine office, both that of the day and that of the night, with great devotion, reciting each hour at the proper time, omitting nothing. And after compline, when he was travelling, he kept silence, and made his companions do the same, just as if they had been in the priory.

Witness I, n. 2

"The same witness said that he (St Dominic) spent the greater part of the night in prayer, and very often the whole night, and that he wept much when he prayed. When asked how he knew this, the witness replied that he had often come across him in the oratory praying and shedding tears, and sometimes, when overcome by slumber, sleeping, and that he very often fell asleep at table because of his vigils at night.

Witness I, n. 5

"Another witness said that his (St Dominic's) custom was always to speak of God or with God, at home, and outside when travelling, and that he encouraged the brethren to do the same, and also put this into the Constitutions. And he said that he knew this because he had seen it, and been there, and heard it, and lived with him. He also said that he (St Dominic) was constant and devout in prayer beyond any other man whom he had ever known. His custom was, as the witness asserted that he had seen, after compline, and after the brethren had made their prayer together, to make them go to the dormitory while he himself remained in the church praying; and at night, while he prayed, he broke out into such sighs and emitted such groans that the brethren, being nearby, were woken up, and some of them were moved to tears. And very often he spent the whole night in prayer, until matins, and nevertheless was present for matins and would go from one side of the choir to the other, admonishing them and urging them to sing up and to sing with devotion.

"Again, the witness said that he had often seen him say Mass, and that in the canon of the Mass, he always saw his eyes and cheeks damp with tears. And he celebrated, and recited the *Pater Noster* at Mass with such devotion, that those present could easily perceive his devotion. And he never remembers having seen him celebrating Mass and not having been thus moved to tears."

Witness 7, n. 3–4

Of the fervour of the first brethren

"No one can possibly recount the fervour that existed in the first days of the Order. . . You would have seen a marvellous fervour throughout the Order. Some brethren would be mourning over their sins and those of others, following their daily and pure confessions with protracted sighs, bitter tears and great cries; others used to join the night to the day by their prayers, making hundreds upon hundreds of genuflections.

"You would have seen our churches rarely or never without some brethren praying there. If brethren were wanted by the porter, they would be more likely to be found praying in the church than anywhere else [...] Many of them who were kindled with this holy fervour used not to rise from prayer until they had obtained some special grace.

"At this same period, the brethren used to look forward to compline as to a festivity, commending themselves to one another with affectionate hearts. No sooner had the bell rung for compline, than the brethren would hurry from wherever they were into choir; and when the office was over, and they had devoutly greeted the Queen of all the world and the Advocate of our Order, they would take the discipline severely. After that, they would make a kind of pilgrimage from one altar to another, humbly prostrating themselves, and bringing forth such rivers of tears that, had you been an outsider, you would have supposed that there was a corpse in the middle of them who was being wept over. Many seculars heard about this and went and witnessed it for themselves, and were extremely edified, which caused some of them to enter the Order [...]

"As for their devotion toward the Blessed Virgin — who can describe it? After they had said the matins of the little Office, standing, and with devotion, they would run with even more devotion to her altar, so that not even the briefest space of time might be devoid of prayer. After matins and compline, they would surround the altar of the Blessed Virgin three-deep, commending themselves and the Order to their Lady. In their cells, also, they had an image of her and of her crucified Son, so that reading and praying and resting they might look upon them, and be looked upon by them in turn with the eye of love."

Gerard de Frachet, Lives of the Brethren, IV, c.1

"From how many brothers did not this holy praise of the glorious Mother of Christ bring forth tears of devotion! A multitude, both of those who chanted and of those who heard them chant, felt their hard hearts soften and melt with love, and burn with piety. Should we not believe that the Mother of our Redeemer is delighted and charmed with such praises and encomiums? A certain man of God, a religious man and worthy of credit, told me that he had often seen in spirit the Mother of our Lord prostrate before the presence of her Son, and praying for the preservation of the whole Order, as the brethren sang, *Eia, ergo, advocata nostra.* We have recorded these things in order that the brethren who read them may be inspired to praise the Virgin with greater devotion henceforth."

Blessed Jordan of Saxony, On the beginnings of the Order, c.63

CPSIA information can be obtained
at www.ICGtesting.com
Printed in the USA
FSHW010213211020
74923FS